ABRAHAM LINCOLN
FRIEND OF THE PEOPLE

• CLARA INGRAM JUDSON •

young
voyageur

Quarto is the authority on a wide range of topics.
Quarto educates, entertains and enriches the lives of
our readers—enthusiasts and lovers of hands-on living.
www.quartoknows.com

© 2016 Quarto Publishing Group USA Inc.
New text © 2016 Quarto Publishing Group USA Inc.
Original text © 1950 Clara Ingram Judson
Additional material © 2007 Flying Point Press
Map © Richard Thompson, Creative Freelancers, Inc.

First published in 1950 by Wilcox and Follett Co. This edition published
in 2016 by Voyageur Press, an imprint of Quarto Publishing Group USA
Inc., 400 First Avenue North, Suite 400, Minneapolis, MN 55401 USA.
Telephone: (612) 344-8100 Fax: (612) 344-8692

quartoknows.com
Visit our blogs at quartoknows.com

Voyageur Press titles are also available at discounts in bulk quantity for
industrial or sales-promotional use. For details contact the Special Sales
Manager at Quarto Publishing Group USA Inc., 400 First Avenue North,
Suite 400, Minneapolis, MN 55401 USA.

10 9 8 7 6 5 4 3 2 1

ISBN: 978-0-7603-5225-0

Library of Congress Control Number: 2016945703

Series Design: B. Middleworth
Series Creative Director: Laura Drew
Page Layout: B. Middleworth

CONTENTS

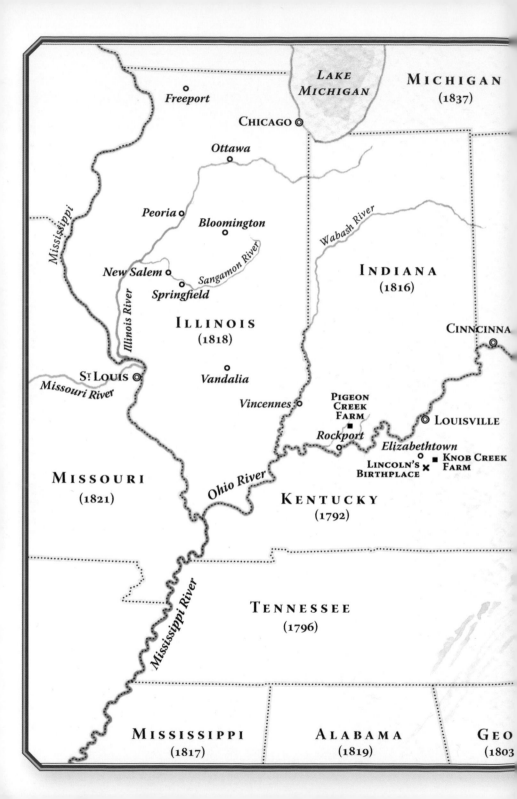

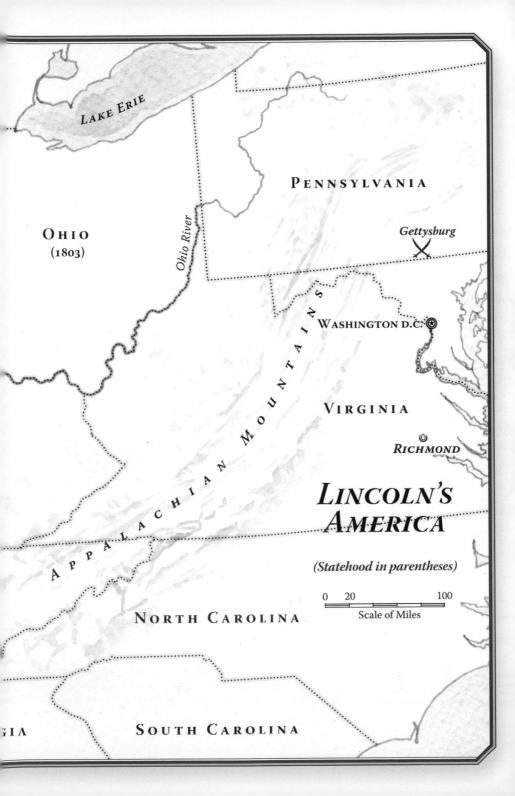

LAKE ERIE

PENNSYLVANIA

OHIO
(1803)

Ohio River

Gettysburg

WASHINGTON D.C.

VIRGINIA

RICHMOND

LINCOLN'S
AMERICA

(Statehood in parentheses)

A P P A L A C H I A N   M O U N T A I N S

0   20   100
Scale of Miles

NORTH CAROLINA

GIA

SOUTH CAROLINA

CHAPTER ONE

FARM BOY

The pungent scent of newly plowed soil hung over the small field. On the hills dogwood and redbud blossoms glistened in the sunshine. Forest trees towered over hepaticas and spring beauties. Cardinals and indigo buntings darted about in the thick underbrush while overhead a hawk hovered, searching confidently. The Kentucky woods were full of game in this spring of 1813.

A man and a boy were walking across the field along a freshly turned furrow.

The Kentucky woods in the fall.

The man, Thomas Lincoln, was of medium height and stocky build; his buckskin breeches were tucked into worn boots and his homespun shirt was shabby. Strong hands were stained with the copper-colored soil and his hair was uncombed. A bulging sack hung from his left shoulder; he reached into it at regular intervals for kernels of corn which he dropped into the open furrow.

The boy had heavy black hair like his father's. His only garment was a long shirt of linsey-woolsey that flapped against his skinny legs as he walked a little behind his father.

"Mind what yer doin', Abe," the man warned; "pumpkins are nice, but I don' want too many vines a-crowdin' out the corn. You keep a-watchin' me an' countin' 'one-two-three' between yer plantin'."

"One-two-three—I drapped one, Pappy," the boy boasted. "I'll not plant too many."

"See that yer don't," Lincoln warned over his shoulder as they tramped on.

At the end of the furrow the man turned.

"We couldn't a had a better day fer plantin'," he remarked agreeably. Then he spied the hawk. "The woods air full of rabbits this spring, Abe. You'n me's goin' huntin' soon as we git this field planted."

"Kaint we go now?" Abe asked eagerly. His father had been working in the fields for several days and meals without fresh meat were monotonous.

"Not yet," Lincoln told his son firmly. "An' no use yer looking sour, Abe. You like corn pone, don't ye?"

"I sure do!" Abe exclaimed, astonished at the question. His stomach under his flapping shirt had felt empty for an hour and the field was not half planted.

"The onlyest way we kin git corn fer meal is to plant it," Lincoln said. "A four-year-old ought to know that. Now git to work." They started planting again.

Thomas Lincoln spoke firmly, for he had to drive himself as well as Abe to do farm work. He much preferred making things. Thomas had had a dreary boyhood hiring out to any farmer who would take him. When he was grown, he chanced to come to Elizabethtown in central Kentucky. There he met the carpenter Joseph Hanks, who liked the youth and taught him the carpenter trade. In 1806 Thomas Lincoln married Joseph Hanks's niece, Nancy Hanks, and the young couple went to housekeeping in Elizabethtown. Thomas had plenty of work because he was skillful at his trade, and their prospects seemed good.

But Lincoln found he did not like town life as well as he had expected. So after the Lincolns' daughter Sarah was born, he suddenly bought a farm a few miles to the south, near Hodgen's mill, and moved his family to the one-room cabin on the land. This place was known as the Sinking Spring farm because of a deep-set spring which bubbled up from under great rocks near the cabin. Here on the twelfth day of February in the year 1809 their son Abraham was born.

Sinking Spring farm was attractive to look at, but not a good place to live; the soil was poor, and the location was very lonely. So Thomas Lincoln decided to move again. His

Corn fields in the afternoon light.

son was two years old before he found what he wanted—a good piece of land by Knob Creek on the main road between Nashville and Louisville. Nearly half of this rich land could be farmed.

The rest was spread over wooded hills that would furnish plenty of firewood, and along the side of one field there was a tiny creek that gave good water. This was the childhood home that Abraham Lincoln remembered and often mentioned.

When the Lincolns moved to Knob Creek farm they furnished the one-room cabin with the usual furniture of that day in Kentucky. There was a post-bed for the parents, made by setting a post into the dirt floor near a corner of the room and placing two long planks from this post to the log walls. Homespun twine laced from wall pegs to the longer board made a base on which was spread a mattress filled with dried cornhusks. The children slept on husk-filled mattresses laid on the floor. These were kept under the big bed in the daytime.

Bedding was dressed skins of buffalo and foxes, home-woven blankets, and quilts. When they moved, the Lincolns could not take all their furniture with them. So in the evenings and on rainy days Thomas Lincoln made new furniture—a table, two splint-bottom chairs, benches, a corner cupboard, and a shelf over the fireplace for the clock. By planting time, two years later, the cabin seemed very comfortable. Lincoln planned to split logs for a puncheon floor and make a better door someday. Pioneers did not expect to have everything quickly.

The stone fireplace was the center of family life, and fire for cooking and for light was kept going all the year around. The woodpile was outside to the left of the door, handy in bad weather. Kitchen utensils hung conveniently at each side of the fireplace, and the spinning wheel and loom were nearby. Knives, pewter forks, and spoons and dishes were kept in the corner cupboard. Strings of dried pumpkin, apples, ears of corn, and herbs for seasoning hung from the ceiling. Mrs. Lincoln cooked meat in a pot that hung from a crane and could be swung over the fire; and she baked corn pones on a smooth plank on the hearth.

On this spring morning as Abe and his father finished planting, Abe ran to the cabin. He knew his mother would have food ready for him. As he came near he saw that blankets, dresses, and shirts were spread over bushes to dry in the hot sun, and he remembered that his mother and Sarah were doing a big washing. But she had baked, too. He could smell the fragrance of the toasting corn meal before he went inside.

"Hungry, Abe?" his mother asked him, teasingly. "Your pones air ready on the hearth. You kin eat now, too, Sarah," she said to her daughter. "I reckon you're both tired enough to sit."

She watched them affectionately; her sallow face—long, like Abe's—looked attractive when she smiled. Nancy Hanks Lincoln was slender and of medium height. Her dark brown hair was coiled in a knot, low on her head, and held in place by a comb carved from a steer's horn. Her linsey-woolsey dress hung straight from her shoulders without hooks or buttons—pioneer women seldom had such luxuries. She waited till the children were settled on the woodpile; then she went into the cabin.

This woodpile was a fine place from which to watch for passing travelers. Sometimes as many as four or five went by in one day. They seemed to appear suddenly from around the hill, and watching for them was fun. Today the pones were almost eaten when Sarah nudged Abe excitedly.

"Look, Abe!" she whispered. "Look 't."

Abe looked beyond her pointing finger as an elegantly dressed man on horseback came into full view from behind the hill. The traveler wore a tall hat of beaver fur, a smartly cut coat, short breeches, stockings, and shoes with big silver buckles.

"Mammy! *Come!*" Sarah called as she slid down from the woodpile and ran to fetch her mother.

"That man's a lawyer," Mrs. Lincoln said when she saw him. "See how his hair is tied back nice? See his fine clothes? Likely he's goin' to court in Elizabethtown. I've seen lawyers there at court-time but never any grander than that one. A lawyer is a great man, children; he kin read 'n write, and he knows the law of the land," she added in a tone of respect.

The three Lincolns watched in silence as the man rode by. He did not glance in their direction. Behind him, on a smaller horse, rode his servant, weighted down with heavy saddlebags and a portmanteau. In his hand the servant carried a tall silk hat. This man turned to grin at the children, but he did not speak.

"Must be somethin' t' be a lawyer," Sarah remarked, feeling snubbed. Most travelers either stopped to chat or shouted greetings as they went by.

Abe did not reply. He slid from the woodpile to fetch more corn pones. Sarah decided scornfully that he was too young to be interested in anything but food.

"Likely he never cared about seein' that lawyer," she thought. "Jes' al'ays hungry."

In a few days all the fields were planted, and after daily chores were done, Sarah and Abe helped their mother dig greens and plant a small garden back of the cabin. By the time that was done, spears of green corn had thrust through the ground and honeysuckle scented the hillsides. Soon it was summer, and the children hunted berries, helped to make soap, and later gathered wild apples for apple butter cooked out of doors in a big kettle.

At harvest time Mrs. Lincoln's cousin, Dennis Hanks, came from town to help with the work. Dennis was fifteen years old, a strong, jolly youth and not uppity about playing and working with the younger Sarah and Abe. He liked stories and jokes, and evenings he encouraged Thomas Lincoln to tell tales of his boyhood.

On a rainy evening a few days after Dennis came, the family were snug in the cabin. Mrs. Lincoln was spinning wool in the corner; Sarah, on a log stool by the hearth, was knitting a sock; and the others sat before the cheerful fire. Raindrops splashed down the chimney and sizzled on hot coals, making the people feel safe and cozy inside the cabin.

"Tell us 'bout yer pappy, tonight," Dennis begged.

"You've heard that tale," Thomas Lincoln grinned at him, liking to be coaxed.

"Hit's a good tale to hear often," Mrs. Lincoln remarked. "Shows how lucky we air now." Lincoln chuckled and leaned forward, ready to talk.

"My pappy was Abraham Lincoln of Virginny—don' you ever forgit you're named after him, Abe. He was a good man. Along about 1784 Pappy set out from Virginny with his wife and five children—I was the youngest son. He'd heard that Kentuck' was a good place, and he meant to git thar."

"Hadn't he ever heard of Indians?" Dennis asked.

"I reckon not," Lincoln replied. "In Virginny he jes' heard that Kentuck' was like paradise and that he could git plenty of land. Leas' wise, that's the way my brother told me. Remember I was only six, then. My brother said Pappy was a real American. His folks was Quaker and come out from England nigh two hundred years before—you kin al'ays be proud of the kin behind you, Abe," he added, glancing at the listening boy.

"We come through the Cumberland Gap to a place Pappy liked, and he settled thar. Hit was nice. We liked hit fine and Pappy built a cabin. One day my brothers was buildin' a fence and me and my pappy was plantin' corn—jes like you an' me planted last spring, Abe—when I heard a yell. Pappy fell down an' rolled over, and I saw an arrow stickin' outa his back.

"Mordecai, my older brother, yelled: 'Josiah! Run fer the fort! Fetch help!' And Josiah started runnin'. Mordecai dashed fer the cabin and got the loaded gun Pappy kept hangin' there. He stuck hit through the window to shoot—but he saw me, bendin' over Pappy. Mordecai had the sense to hold his fire, though hit was hard. He could see an Indian come creepin', creepin', from behind a tree to git Pappy's scalp. Mordecai took keerful aim fer a bright silver bangle over that savage heart, and then he fired.

"Bout killed me, that racket did. The Indian fell over me an' Pappy. Mordecai come runnin' an' pulled me out. The Indian was dead. After while help came from the fort. Those men stayed 'round. They killed two more Indians and buried Pappy. Then Mammy and us had to git on best way we could—but we made out."

"An' now you're here, Pappy," Abe said, and he sighed in sleepy content.

The fire had burned low. Raindrops still spattered. But the cabin felt warm and comfortable as the children pulled out pallets and went to bed.

CHAPTER TWO

KENTUCKY SCHOOL

Two years went by, all so run together in Abe Lincoln's mind that afterwards he couldn't tell which year was which. Dennis Hanks liked Knob Creek farm and came so often that he seemed like one of the Lincoln family. But he was not there on a chilly day early in 1815 when Thomas Lincoln arrived home with news.

"Schoolmaster Riney's openin' a school three miles up the pike," he remarked.

"A school! Oh, *Thomas!*" Mrs. Lincoln exclaimed and her eyes sparkled joyfully. "The children kin go, kaint they?"

An old schoolhouse.

"I don' know as they need schoolin'," he replied. She watched him anxiously as he took off heavy shoes and stretched his feet to the fire. "I kaint read, ner write more'n my name, and I git along fine. What's readin' goin' to git a person?"

"But Thomas, readin's nice," Mrs. Lincoln protested. "I al'ays wanted the children to learn to read."

"Well, they're goin' t' git their chance," Lincoln said teasingly. "I've paid fer six weeks of schoolin' for 'em already."

"Abe an' me go to school, Pappy?" Sarah exclaimed. Abe saw that his mother had flushed and looked happy, and smiled at her husband gratefully.

Mrs. Lincoln had to work hard to get them ready for school by Monday. Sarah needed a dress, and his mother made Abe his first pair of breeches. When he tried them on he paraded in front of the fire proudly, showing them off.

"They're jes' like Pappy's!" he gloated. "Look, Sarah, I've got breeches like Pappy's." Sarah grinned, knowing that he had wanted man-clothes. The Lincoln children looked nice when their father took them to the new school.

At that time there were no public schools in Kentucky. Parents paid tuition in food or clothing or cash if they had any. Schoolmaster Riney taught a "blab school"—a name which meant that pupils "blabbed" (talked out loud while they memorized lessons) so that the teacher could know they were studying. The Knob Creek school was a shabby one-room cabin. A log left out of one wall let in light. Riney used Dilworth's Spelling Book—the famous "Blue-Backed

Speller"—and he stood over the dozen children, switch in hand, to make sure they worked. The room was full of sound, but Abe saw that Riney could not be fooled; he knew in a moment if a pupil stopped blabbing, and he went after that one with his switch.

When Sarah and Abe got home the first day their mother had hot pones ready for them and was eager to hear what they had learned. That night, after Abe had curled up under a buffalo skin he whispered the lesson, "a, b, c—" softly, so as not to waken his father.

"That you, Abe?" his mother whispered. "You sick?" "No, Mammy," Abe replied, "jest sayin' the lesson."

She got up and covered him snugly. "You must learn hard whilst you have the chanct, Abe," she said. "Learnin's good!"

Sarah and Abe learned the alphabet, to spell a few words, and that two and two make four. Older children had writing lessons and used homemade quills and sumac-juice ink. Abe was just starting to make letters with a charcoal stick on a split log when the school closed. Children were needed at their homes for the spring work.

At the Knob Creek farm, Abe now rode the horse while his father held the bull-tongue plow to a straight furrow. Thomas Lincoln was doing well on this rich land. He now had four horses, a cow, pigs, and some sheep; a boy could help a lot caring for the animals. After the planting, Abe weeded the potato patch and chopped firewood.

"You larn to knock up kindlin' fer yer mammy, and soon I'll teach you to chop down a tree," his father promised.

After the chores were done, Abe fished or looked for honey, berries, or nuts according to the season. The Kentucky woods furnished many kinds of food for people who would gather it.

Sarah had her chores, too. She set the table with wooden bowls and cups her father had made, and after the meal she washed them and put them away. Their few crockery dishes were kept on a higher shelf, for company use. Sarah polished the knives and the pewter forks and spoons with sand that Abe fetched from the creek; and she rubbed the copper kettle till it shone. She milked the cow and helped Abe pull weeds and knitted socks; and this year Mrs. Lincoln had taught her to card wool shorn from their own sheep.

The father and mother worked hard; making a living was a family enterprise. Thomas Lincoln planted fields and harvested. He hunted for game and took the corn to Hogden's mill to be ground into meal. He built fences and a shelter for his stock, and in the winter he did carpentering jobs for neighbors.

Mrs. Lincoln sewed and cooked and spun and wove cloth on her loom. She was a good seamstress and clothes she made hung better than many "best" clothes worn to church. In her spare time she pieced a coverlet that looked nice on the bed, daytimes. She was a good cook and knew which herbs to gather in the woods to make a tasty stew.

Abe liked to watch her make corn pone. She mixed meal and water in a bowl and then molded the cakes between the palms of her hands. A quick press when it was shaped put a

Corn pone is very similar to the skillet cornbread we eat today.

print of her palm on the cake—"Nancy's print" she called it, smiling as she set the pones on the hearth to bake.

Afternoons, when her work was done and there was time before she must get supper, she took a splint-bottom chair outside and leaned against the cabin to rest. Sarah and Abe loved that hour. She sang to them or told tales about life in town. Some folks had slaves to do the work for them, she said, and fine clothes and a carriage to take them around. These stories did not make her or the children feel "poor"; they were just tales and fun to hear. People feel "rich" or "poor" in comparison with their neighbors. The Lincolns were comfortable enough according to standards around Knob Creek.

On stormy days Mrs. Lincoln rested by the fireplace. Often she took the small Bible from the shelf and read a story to the children. She read poorly. Abe liked it better when she found a place and a name to remind her and then told the story in her own words. Occasionally she was quiet and sad. Perhaps she grieved for the baby brother who was born and died before Abe could remember.

Life was not all work in Kentucky. The Lincolns had friends. People got together for house-raisings and cornhuskings and weddings and funerals, and most families went to church. The Lincolns belonged to the Little Mount Church a few miles away. Abe and his father rode one horse to meetings, and Sarah and her mother rode the other. Each summer there was a big camp meeting that lasted several days. Farmers put their stock into a fenced-in field and let the animals look after themselves. Camp meetings were noisy and jolly as well as religious; people needed that kind of a change after months on their lonely farms.

These Kentucky pioneers spoke a dialect of their own, though they called it English. The first of anything was the *fust*. Mr. Lincoln said, "The pigs *air* in the garden," and Mrs. Lincoln told Sarah to be *keerful* when she washed crockery dishes. When Mr. Lincoln went to town he *brung* back things. Abe *drapped* seeds and went to school to be *eddicated*. Even the Lincoln name was pronounced and spelled many ways— Linkhorn, Linkern, Linkun. Pioneers were independent people; they talked as they pleased with no bother about a dictionary.

The only way Abe learned about the world beyond the hills was through the travelers who now and then stopped at the cabin to eat or to sleep. At such times the men talked by the fire. The names of people they mentioned were fascinating to hear—Napoleon, Astor, Boone, Tecumseh. Abe often said them over afterwards, relishing the sounds. Sometimes the men spoke of "the United States" and a "flag."

"I got a flag of my own," a visitor boasted one winter evening. He pulled a bit of cloth from under his shirt and proudly unfurled it. Abe saw that it was a pretty thing—red and white and blue with stars. "All eighteen stars, for eighteen states," the owner pointed out. Eighteen was higher than Abe could count at that time.

The men talked about "freedom" and "slavery" and "Virginny"—and praised a young man from Kentucky, Henry Clay, who was making a name for himself, they said. Sometimes they talked in a worried way about "titles" and "surveys" and "taxes" and the "law." These words interested Abe long before he knew the meanings. One night he heard his father say, "Well, I don' need to worry none. I got title to my land and my taxes is paid." The men said he was lucky.

Early in 1816 another school started, and Abe was glad to go. Maybe now he would learn the meaning of some of those words; his father never liked explaining. But that school closed too when planting time came. Dennis Hanks arrived the next week, and the annual round of work began again.

On an autumn evening of that year, 1816, Thomas Lincoln looked cross and weary when he returned from a trip to town. Abe helped him feed and bed the horse, but no word was spoken. His father didn't notice the good supper, which the children ate with eager pleasure. He sat with drooping shoulders and cast occasional sad glances around the cheerful room.

Indiana farmland.

"This's been a nice home," he remarked presently.

"We like it right well," his wife agreed, thinking to comfort him.

"But Kentuck''s no place fer us," Lincoln continued. "We ought 'er move."

Abe was so astonished that he stopped chewing a mouthful of pone and honey. His mother waited anxiously.

"I bought my land here and thought my title was good,"

Lincoln went on after a painful silence. "I paid my taxes and I've got my papers." He scowled at his family as though they had made his misery. "And now I git a paper that says I'm a trespasser. I'm sued fer trespassin' on my own land!"

"How could that be, Thomas?" His wife was puzzled.

"Seems like that's the way it is in Kentuck' now. In the early days settlers took land where they pleased—my own pappy did, Mordecai said. Land offices were a long way off— no tellin' where. Then, like as not, a settler picked up and went on west. And maybe another man came and took that same land. Seems that a man's come back here now and says my land was his'n. The lawyer says I've got a good claim 'cause I paid, and I could fight back. But I hain't a-goin' to—not when I've paid a'ready." The three at the table watched him, puzzled by this mysterious tragedy.

"I heard today that in Indianny a man kin buy land straight from the government at two dollars an acre and no worry about a title—" Abe started to interrupt and his father said, "A title's a paper that says a settler has a right to the land he paid fer, son, and it's mighty important.

"I say I'm tired of frettin'. We should leave this farm! I'll not stay here and fight fer the title. My brother Josiah moved to Indianny. If he kin, we kin. I say we move—what do you say, Nancy?" He turned to his wife eagerly.

"I'll go wherever you go, Thomas," Nancy Lincoln answered. "Now you eat—you're wore out."

CHAPTER THREE

ACROSS THE WIDE OHIO

The next time Thomas Lincoln went to town he told friends he was leaving; soon he began to build a flatboat for his journey to Indiana. Abe went with him every day to the place where Knob Creek entered Rolling Fork, two and a half miles from the cabin, and there they worked on the boat until dark. A boy who was going on eight could help in many ways. He fetched tools; he learned to chop smaller branches from a tree trunk; and he could help drag a log and float it on the river.

A farmhouse at the Coalins Forest and Game Reservation, between the Tennessee and Cumberland Rivers in Kentucky.

The boat was to be like a raft, with a light railing at the sides. When it was finished, Sarah and her mother helped carry things from the cabin: the cupboard, the plow, the tool chest, and other supplies for loading.

On a bright autumn day, Thomas Lincoln poled away, alone. He would float down Rolling Fork, down Salt River, and to the Ohio; and then across to Indiana. When he had drifted out of sight, his family turned and walked home. It would be a long time before they could expect to see him again.

But the days went by quickly for Sarah and Abe. Several neighbors came to say good-bye—the Brownfields, the Gollahers, the Thompsons, the Ashcrafts, and others. Sarah helped her mother do a big washing—so bedding and clothing would be clean for the move. Abe gathered nuts and fished and kept the woodpile supplied. Mrs. Lincoln made a new quilt and packed her dishes in it and put them in a sack.

Then one afternoon, Thomas Lincoln stood at the door— so brown, so happy that he had not minded the long walk back to Knob Creek. Mrs. Lincoln hurried to get him a good supper, but the children asked so many questions he could hardly find time to eat it.

"Yes, I found us a place, Sarah," he grinned at her.

"Yes, I had a fine trip, Abe."

"Wait now, till yer pappy's et," Mrs. Lincoln told them, smiling at their eagerness. "Then he can tell it all."

After supper they sat by the hearth to listen. Abe built a big fire; he was proud to show his father that there was plenty of wood handy. Then Thomas Lincoln told his story.

"I made out fine on Rollin' Fork an' Salt River—jest floatin' an' polin' along easy," he recounted. "But when I come to that Ohio—such a river as that is! The current was stronger than hit looked to be. My boat caught on a snag— er somethin' —and next I knowed my tool chest, an' yer cupboard, Nancy, had slid into the river."

"Ye lost 'em, Pappy!" Abe exclaimed. Mrs. Lincoln's face was suddenly white.

"Not me!" Lincoln laughed in a masterful way. "I waded in and fetched up everythin'. I was glad to git my tools—I'd hate to lose them.

"Finally I got across the Ohio and landed near Anderson's Creek in Indianny. I left my things with a man named Francis Posey—he looked like a good man—and I set off to hunt us a farm."

He talked all evening. The eager listeners inspired him to recall amusing incidents, which he told well. From Posey's he had walked sixteen miles northwest along an old buffalo trail through deep forest. One day he came to a pretty knoll where the trees stood a little more apart.

"I knowed right off that was the place fer us," Lincoln boasted proudly. "I'd carried my small ax so I notched trees and piled brush to mark the place. We'll have a hundred an' sixty acres, Nancy, and the government gives us time to pay fer hit. Thar'll be a job, clearing fields fer corn, but the woods air full of game an' the soil's fine.'

"Kin we start tomorry?" Abe begged.

"You ready, Nancy?" Lincoln asked his wife. "I oughter git a shelter built before bitter weather sets in."

"I need a day fer cooking up food," Mrs. Lincoln reminded him. "We could start the mornin' after."

In the morning Lincoln butchered a hog, and busied himself packing the things they were to take with them. Mrs. Lincoln fried the hog meat and made a basketful of corn pones. The children helped to pack the saddlebags. That long-handled frying pan she called a "spider" was hard to fit in, but she couldn't leave it behind. They were forced to discard many things they really needed.

At dawn the next day, early in December of 1816, the Lincoln family left Knob Creek farm. Abe and his father were to ride one horse and Sarah and her mother the other. But the loads were so heavy that the grownups walked most of the hundred-mile journey. At night they camped in the woods.

Abe stared incredulously when they reached the Ohio River—he had never seen so much water in his life. And something was going by all the time—uprooted trees, canoes, flatboats, one after the other! The Lincolns crossed safely on Thompson's ferry and entered Indiana the same month it became a state in the Union.

That year, 1816, seemed to mark a change in the young United States, though at the time people didn't suspect it. The wars for independence were over; new, vigorous leaders were replacing the men who had planned the republic and had written the Constitution. The acquisition of the Floridas and the vast undefined tract of land across the Mississippi River called "Louisiana" opened new vistas to Americans who had not satisfied their ambitions in the East. People were moving

A wagon train of men, women, and children moving through the mountains.

as never before in history, thousands of people—men, women, boys, and girls.

Many left Europe and came to the United States to get more land and a chance to live a better life. Sailing ships were packed; and some of these immigrants crossed the mountains and then floated down the Ohio in their search for new homes. The river was the great highway to the West. It was easier for travel than the Great Lakes or the trip around the Gulf of Mexico. Few thought of stopping in Indiana at the time the Lincolns ferried over—the forests were thick and forbidding.

Not all people who moved came to the United States by their own wish. Black people were stolen and brought across the sea to be slaves. White people were kidnapped or tricked and found themselves "indentured servants"—doomed to work for years until their "time was up" and they had earned the high cost of their forced passage. Flatboats that drifted by

Thompson's ferry carried many kinds of people. Abe thought the river was interesting.

Thomas Lincoln found Mr. Posey, who greeted them cordially and loaned them a wagon with runners instead of wheels for their journey through the forest. Lincoln bought a cow, and Posey gave Abe a dog for company. Then he helped them load their things and wished them luck on the way.

Abe walked with his father, or ran ahead as his dog chased squirrels, 'possums, raccoons, and wild turkeys. The Lincolns had never seen such a forest. Elms, sycamores, white oaks, and beechnut, hickory, and walnut trees towered high. Thick vines twined from tree to tree, shutting out light even in the winter. Posey had warned them about panthers, bears, and wolves so they watched with anxious care.

On the third day they crossed pretty little Pigeon Creek.

"Better drink yer fill here," Lincoln remarked. "I haint found water nigher our place yet." So they drank and washed their hands and feet.

At the top of the next rise Lincoln paused. "Now yer on our land," he said proudly. "I say we eat."

They hurriedly unloaded some things. Each knew what to do. Lincoln killed a wild turkey; Abe built a fire; Sarah hunted a thin flat stone and put it to heat by the flames; and Mrs. Lincoln made corn pones with meal they had bought from Posey. It was wonderful to know that the long journey was ended.

The next morning Thomas Lincoln began to build their shelter. He planned a "half-faced camp," the kind often used in sugar camps. First he selected two trees about fifteen feet apart east to west; and then he set a post some ten feet north of each tree. These four were the corner posts, which he connected with saplings. More saplings laid across made the support for the roof of piled-on brush. While he worked with posts and saplings, the others collected brush, enough for the roof and to pile around three sides. In front they would keep a fire going night and day, for heat and cooking and to keep off wild beasts. Often at night the terrifying shriek of a panther awakened them. Abe never forgot that sound nor their fear that some beast might prowl into their camp.

The Lincolns lived this way for nearly a year, and they were seldom comfortable. The fire used up wood fast, and it was Abe's chore to keep plenty close by. North winds blew the heat away. South winds sent smoke and embers inside. But Thomas Lincoln had no time to build better; he had to clear a space in the forest for spring planting. This work was hardly begun when they discovered a new difficulty.

In the fall, when Lincoln had walked from Posey's, he had seen many good springs; but now he couldn't find one on his own land. He dug pits to hold snow or rain water, Mrs. Lincoln melted snow in the kettle, and the children filled pails at the spring. At first it was fun to see who could carry the most—but with the spring a mile away, the pleasure of that game didn't last long. They simply learned to do with less water.

Life was easier when warmer weather came. The forest was beautiful with blossoms—wild crab, redbud, dogwood, and a ground covering of lavender phlox. Later Sarah picked buttercups and swamp lilies and iris near the creek; wild roses bloomed and honeysuckle scented the woods as in Kentucky. But by June, Abe had to keep a smoke fire going night and day to protect them from hordes of mosquitoes and flies.

Through all this the Lincolns had missed the help and company of Dennis Hanks, and it was a happy day when he arrived from Kentucky to stay. Work went faster now. Planting was finished, and more land was cleared. With logs from the trees he cut down, Lincoln started building a cabin.

After the 1817 harvest Lincoln went to Elizabethtown to collect payments due to him, and he brought back Mrs. Lincoln's aunt and uncle, the Thomas Sparrows, and news of Kentucky. The title of his farm was not settled yet. New people were moving to Kentucky now. Henry Clay was sent to Congress again and was Speaker of the House—a high honor, townspeople had boasted. Deep in the forest, the Lincolns had little interest in such outside news. Small home happenings were more important.

The men hurried to roof the new cabin because the Sparrows were to live in the old camp until Uncle could build his cabin. Sarah and Abe marveled at the size of their new home. It was eighteen by twenty feet, larger than any cabin they had lived in. Lincoln built a loft overhead—reached by ladderlike pegs set in the wall—and Abe and Dennis slept there. The fireplace was wide, and the stick-and-mud chimney drew well. Someday they would have a floor and a door and a window. The Lincolns felt that they were doing well.

Then, suddenly, a mysterious and deadly illness appeared in the Pigeon Creek neighborhood. It was called "milksick" because both cows and people got it and died after a short illness. Thomas Sparrow and his wife died, and a few days later Mrs. Lincoln sickened. Sarah made broth—but her mother could not eat. Abe fetched fresh water—but she could not drink. Terror clutched them. They could not look at each other or speak. Abe could hardly swallow because of the great lump in his throat.

On a golden afternoon in October of 1818, Nancy Hanks Lincoln died. Abe felt numb, as though the whole world had suddenly stopped. His mother dead? The words his father spoke had no meaning to him.

Thomas Lincoln turned from the bedside and went outdoors. He got his saw and cut planks from a fine log that he had chosen for flooring in the new cabin. Dennis smoothed the boards and Abe silently whittled locust pegs for nails. When the coffin was made, Sarah lined it with the best coverlet, spreading it neatly as her mother would have liked. Together they buried Abe's mother at the edge of the dark forest. And now there were three graves on that small knoll.

Abe Lincoln was nine at this time—going on ten. He had loved his mother dearly and without her he was very lonely.

• CHAPTER FOUR •

A NEW FAMILY

After that day Thomas Lincoln had hours of silent grieving that frightened his children. He sat by the hearth brooding, his head bowed. Often Abe wandered into the woods and sat on a log alone, thinking. His mother had taught him about God and had read from her Bible. Now, when he was lonely, "God" seemed just a name to say, and he couldn't find the words that she had read in the Book.

A farm woman.

He missed little things he had hardly noticed before—her smile, the fragrant corn pones she had waiting for him, the new words she had helped him learn.

Sarah, going on twelve, did the best she knew, but nothing tasted right.

"I thought I could cook," she told Abe and Dennis, "but Mammy was right thar. 'Now turn hit,' she'd say, 'don't let hit catch fire!' An' we'd laugh. Now I don't know when hit's *done!*"

Clothes got dirty, but the soap was used up and the creek water was too cold for laundry work. Sarah had milked the Lincolns' two cows, but her mother had made the cheese. Now the bag was too worn to use. Abe tore his shirt and Sarah could not find a needle, though she was sure her mother had had two good ones.

In the spring the forest was beautiful with bloom and occasionally travelers went by. One day a traveling preacher passed; and when he was told of the three deaths, he agreed to wait over night and hold a service. The next morning he prayed and read the Bible by the graves. Abe knew that his mother would have liked that, and the comfort of doing something for her eased a little of his heartache.

A few weeks later Schoolmaster Andrew Crawford started a school about three miles from the Lincoln home. Sarah and Abe went to it for a little while; then it closed and Crawford went away.

Thomas Lincoln roused himself for the spring planting, but evenings when the children begged for stories he sat silent and morose. This dull living went on for about a year.

Then, one fall morning in 1819 he rose with new vigor. Sarah saw that he had washed and combed his hair. Something had surely happened, but she didn't know what it was. He ate a big breakfast and strode off toward Posey's without saying a word to them.

He didn't come back that evening. He didn't come the next day. A fortnight later they still had heard nothing.

The children ate out of doors with no bother about dishes and pans. They had nuts and pawpaws, persimmons, and wild grapes. Abe ground corn with a stone in a hollow stump, and Sarah baked pones by the fire. Dennis snared quail, which they broiled on green sticks. The weather was fine; they seldom went into the cabin by daylight, so they didn't notice how dirty it was.

Their father had been gone for some time, and picnic ways were getting irksome, when on a cool morning Dennis heard wild creatures scampering. The sounds came from the trail to the east. The children paused, listening.

"Someone's comin'," Abe whispered.

"Is that Pappy?" Sarah asked, thinking of the unmade beds. "Reck'n hit's a team," Dennis guessed. Most travelers walked or rode a horse.

"Pappy's got no team," Abe said. They waited, tense with listening.

Soon a strange caravan emerged from the forest. Thomas Lincoln strode ahead guiding a pair of oxen that pulled a covered wagon. A neatly bonneted woman held the reins, and sitting high on chests behind her were three children and a cat that was mewing plaintively. As the wagon drew near, his amazed children saw that Lincoln wore a new coat, had a town haircut, and that he looked happy.

"I brung you a new mammy!" he called, and gestured toward the woman on the wagon. Then he yelled, "Whoa!" to the oxen and helped the stranger down.

Dennis slipped away but Sarah and Abe stood silent, watching her. Probably Thomas Lincoln's children never looked worse. Their days of freedom had left them with uncombed hair and dirty faces, torn clothing and mud-caked feet. The new Mrs. Lincoln had seen all that from a-top the wagon. But as she walked near she saw, too, that Abe was heartsick. With a quick, mothering gesture she put her arm around him and pressed his grimy head against her pretty dress. The tender gesture broke through his loneliness and Abe felt a comfort he had not known for a year.

Before either spoke, the small boy on the wagon shouted to his mother:

"Mama! Kin we git down now?" he asked.

"Yes, John. Help him slide down, Matilda," Mrs. Lincoln answered; then she turned and drew Sarah close as she went on speaking. "Those are my children—Elizabeth, Matilda, and John. You Johnstons come and meet Sarah and Abe Lincoln. And that young man by the tree is Dennis Hanks, their cousin. We are all one big family now. We're going to get on fine," she added, as she stepped to the cabin door.

Thomas Lincoln had been watching her. Now he spoke hastily. "I'll be tendin' my team," he said as he moved away.

"Not till you've fetched water," Mrs. Lincoln called in a firm voice. She had seen the state of that cabin at her first glance. "Maybe you all better help him—I'll need a lot of water. Matilda, bring soap—you know where it's packed. Elizabeth, get the blue dress from the clothes chest. Sarah wears about your size; she'll wear yours until I get to sewing." Her vigorous tone got them moving, and as she talked, she put on a big apron and went to work.

Sarah and Abe were scrubbed from head to toe with hot water and soap. Abe's shaggy locks were neatly trimmed and Sarah's hair was dried with a towel till it had the sheen of a ripe chestnut. As she worked Mrs. Lincoln talked about their journey.

"Didn't your father tell you he was going back to Kentucky?" This amazed her. "Well, I reckon he's been half sick this last year. I knew your father long ago when I was Sarah Bush. Then I married Mr. Johnston, and we had these children. A day or so before going to Kentucky your father chanced to hear from a passing traveler that Mr. Johnston was dead. So he came to Kentucky thinking to marry me." (Abe recalled that traveler, but neither he nor Sarah had guessed that the man had brought news.)

A sound outside made her step to the door; Lincoln was unloading the wagon.

"Leave my things there for the night, Thomas," she said quickly. "I'll not unpack till the cabin is scrubbed. The first thing we need is a floor. You've got some good logs over there; it wouldn't take a smart man like you long to lay a floor and hang a door and a window frame. The floor comes first. We'll camp outside till it is down."

Without further comment she cooked a good supper and talked the children into feeling at home with each other. Abe never knew what she thought about the state of that cabin and his father's probably persuasive accounts of life in Indiana. Sarah Bush Lincoln was a woman of character. She expected to see through a job that she took on and to be a good mother to children that were under her care. Abe liked and respected her, always.

The next morning Thomas Lincoln talked to Dennis and Abe as he sawed logs for that floor. He had collected money due him in Kentucky and with that had bought clothes and paid some small debts of Sarah Johnston's. And then they were married. She owned nice things—they were in the wagon now—but she had little money. It was good for both of them to marry and bring up their families together.

Soon the floor was laid, the door and the window hung, and the furniture put in place. The clean cabin seemed like a palace to Sarah and Abe. The three boys, Dennis, Abe, and John, slept in the loft. The girls had pallets in a corner until Lincoln built a "lean-to" for them. The copper kettle shone now, and candles lighted the supper table. Food was tasty, and life became mannerly again. Abe began to thrive.

Now there was time for him to notice that Mrs. Lincoln had put a few books on a small shelf. Among them he saw *Robinson Crusoe*, *Pilgrim's Progress*, *Sinbad the Sailor*, and *Aesop's Fables*. One day she found him fingering pages; he put the book back hastily.

"Read all you like, Abe," she said kindly. "I'll help you with words you don't know." That evening she remarked to her husband, "Abe ought to go to school. I'd like for all of them to go."

"Not me!" Dennis warned hastily. "I'm growed."

"Sarah and Abe went last year, but it didn't come to much," Lincoln told her, and grinned at Dennis. "Thar warn't enough young'uns to make hit pay."

"Schoolmaster Crawford larnt us nice ways," Sarah remembered. "He had us git up an' come in the door and say 'Howdy' like we was company come t' visit." She acted out entering a room and the Johnston children laughed till they tumbled off their stools.

"I'd rather larn to read an' write," Abe said.

"You shall, Abe," Mrs. Lincoln promised. "And meanwhile you may read my books."

Soon after that talk a new master came to Pigeon Creek, and the children attended school. But he stayed only a short time. A year or more later Azel Dorsey came to the neighborhood and opened a school about four miles from the Lincoln home. Mrs. Lincoln saw to it that all five children started at once.

Azel Dorsey was a good teacher, and it was from him that Abe Lincoln learned to write the fine, even script that he used all his life. From Dorsey, too, Abe got his first training in public speaking. The schoolmaster taught them how to stand and had them recite "pieces" they memorized from Scott's *Lessons in Elocution*, a collection of prose and poetry. The Declaration of Independence was a popular selection for speaking, and it is likely that Abe memorized it at this time. Dorsey's pupils learned arithmetic from Pike's textbook, and the teacher was particular about their spelling.

Each Friday afternoon, school ended with a spelling match. Pupils chose sides and stood in rows along opposite walls. Abe was often the winner, and his rival was pretty Ann Roby.

One afternoon as Ann's turn came, Dorsey called the word "defied."

Glibly Ann began, "D-e-f-"—then she paused, uncertain of the next letter. She glanced wildly toward Abe—if she missed he would win again!

He saw her distress. With his right hand, the one away from the teacher, he pointed to his eye. Ann got his meaning.

"-i-e-d," she finished triumphantly; and the match ended in a tie, as the time was up.

But that school, too, lasted only a short time. But little by little Abe learned to figure simple arithmetic problems, to write, and to read.

Unfortunately, it was not always easy to find time for reading, because Abe's liking for books annoyed his father.

"Ye care more about readin' than workin'," Lincoln complained. Abe grinned. His father spoke truly. Abe liked to read and to think, but he hated physical labor. He was tall and strong now, and he worked along with his father and Dennis. They had cleared eighteen acres and planted corn, potatoes, and wheat; they built rail fences, dug wells (but found no water), and did the daily chores of a pioneer farmer—tending stock, getting firewood, and hunting. Wild game was still the family's main source of meat.

Abe never cared for hunting, but he went along with his father until the day when he shot a turkey. He happened to be in the cabin when, through the door, he spied a handsome wild turkey. He picked up a gun and fired at it. A roar, a loud squawk, a flutter—and the bird lay still. Abe set the gun down and went to fetch the turkey to dress for cooking. As he picked it up, the bird's stillness and its gay plumage, so stained with blood from his act, sickened him. He never went hunting again.

Toting corn to the mill was the only chore that Abe Lincoln really liked. He volunteered for that every time he had a chance. He rode the horse bareback, with the sack of corn laid in front of him. On a horse he had an easy grace that was a contrast to his awkward walk. He wore a coonskin cap, a deerskin shirt, homespun breeches, low shoes, and short socks. His breeches were always too short, perhaps because he was growing so fast. They usually missed his shoes by inches and his bony ankles were often blue with cold.

At the mill he stood around, agreeably, waiting his turn. Men liked the tall youth. He was neither shy, nor too forward, and he began to make friends.

CHAPTER FIVE

SQUIRE PATE AND THE LAW

In the early 1820s many new settlers came to settle in the Pigeon Creek neighborhood. Each new family had to clear and fence fields and build a cabin as the Lincolns had done earlier. They needed extra help, but laborers were scarce because each family had work at home. Naturally newcomers noticed the tall, husky Abe Lincoln, and one day as he waited his turn at the mill, two men offered him jobs. He was perhaps fourteen at this time. Abe laughed and told the men that his pappy needed him. More work was the last thing that Abe Lincoln wanted!

Lincoln takes a break from splitting rails.

But as he jogged home he thought over those offers. Work for hire would be work, the same as at home, and he hated it. But work with different people would be a change; since he had to work anyway, why not try it? Figured this way, the idea seemed good. He resolved that if his father was willing, he would hire out.

Only a few days later a nearby farmer asked Thomas Lincoln about hiring Abe. Lincoln eyed his son thoughtfully; the boy had grown more than Lincoln had realized. It wouldn't be a bad idea to have him bring in some money. Of course Abe's earnings would belong to his father; that was the custom of the time.

"Yes, I reckon Abe kin oblige you soon as the plantin's done here," he decided. "Start next Monday, say."

So Abe began "hiring out." At first he worked two or three days at a time, staying on a job till a certain task was done, then coming home to chop wood or split rails for his father. He earned sixteen cents a day when he felled trees, split rails, dug wells, and helped build cabins. For hog-butchering and snake killing—which he hated—he got twenty-five cents.

Abe proudly carried his own ax to work. He had carved the handle from hardwood; and the head was sharp and heavy, with a point above and below.

"Seems like I've an ax in my hand all the time," he remarked to Matilda one evening as he set it in a corner. "Be sleepin' with it next, I reckon!"

His strength and growth developed together, perhaps because he used his muscles constantly. By the time Abe was sixteen he was six feet four inches tall and the way he could swing that ax was a sight to remember! Often a felled tree cracked loudly and split at a stroke. Word of his prowess got around and he had more jobs offered than he could accept.

When Abe worked nearby, Matilda Johnston was allowed to carry his lunch to him. Sometimes, as she came near, she saw him standing on a stump orating. She amused herself by trying to guess what it was he recited—the Declaration of Independence, the sermon of last Sunday, or a chapter from Isaiah. All of these were favorites. Then she would run to him and ask if her guess was right.

Probably Abe's growing acquaintance helped to draw the Lincoln family into the community, for their life became less lonely. House-raisings, corn huskings, weddings, and funerals brought neighbors together. The Pigeon Creek church, started in 1819, was finally finished; and regular services were well attended. Mr. and Mrs. Lincoln were members, and Thomas Lincoln had made window and door frames and a handsome pulpit as his contribution.

In the spring of 1824, James Gentry, a well-to-do Kentuckian, bought a thousand acres of land about a mile and a half west of the Lincoln farm. When he built a house and a store, he hired Abe Lincoln to help with building and fencing. As they worked together Abe became a friend of Gentry's son, Allen. Later Mr. Gentry trusted Abe to clerk in the store, too, when the Gentrys were busy with other work. Clerking, Abe discovered, was nice work. A person could take his ease between customers.

Mr. Gentry was a shrewd business man and soon observed that men liked his clerk. Abe Lincoln had a friendly way and a ready tale. Customers lingered and sometimes made further purchases.

"Stay around awhile! Take your time!" Gentry would invite. "Abe Lincoln will be here in a minute." To a new man in the county he added, "That boy can make folks laugh over nothing. It isn't *what* he says; it's the way he says it. Get him to tell you how old man Brown got hornswoggled selling hogs." Men stayed around until Abe went home.

A few months later William Jones came from Vincennes and opened a store a mile beyond Gentry's. He was quick to hire Abe, and used him when Gentry could spare him. While doing errands for these men, Abe came to know David Turnham—who had a farm near Grand View—and Attorney John Pitcher, of Rockport—a town eighteen miles southwest and on the Ohio River.

As he went about, Abe Lincoln noticed that most families owned books. Turnham and Pitcher had many; usually there were only a few on a shelf. Often Abe was allowed to borrow a book to read evenings. In this way he read Grimshaw's *History of the United States*, *The Arabian Nights*, Weems's *Life of Washington*, and others. He carried a book in his breeches pocket, and at the slightest excuse he would stop work and read for a few minutes. This habit annoyed his father.

"Where's Abe?" Thomas Lincoln always asked when he came into the cabin.

"He went to Turnham's to borrow a book," Mrs. Lincoln answered casually one day.

"That boy!" Lincoln cried angrily. "He thinks more of readin' than workin'. He's lazy—that's all! I had a job for him." He stalked out of the cabin, his face flushed with anger.

Mrs. Lincoln sighed. Such scenes happened often; it was hard to keep peace. But when Abe came in for supper he had no ill feeling, though his father had scolded.

"Pappy didn't uster fret so," he said in half apology.

"He's had his troubles," Mrs. Lincoln agreed. "A man was here digging again today, but they found no water. Funny, too, with that big marsh so near."

But a time came when Abe's learning helped his father. Thomas Lincoln had a deal to sell eighteen acres of his land. Abe happened to be working near when the buyer brought the paper to be signed, and he glanced at the document.

"Want fer me to look hit over, Pappy?" he asked mildly.

Grudgingly, Lincoln handed the bill of sale to his son. Abe read it carefully; his hunch had been right.

"If you sign this paper, Pappy, you've given him yer whole farm," he said. "Did yer aim to do that?"

"Ye mean he's hornswoggling me!" Lincoln roared. He grabbed the paper and ordered the man off his land. After that Lincoln usually let his son read in peace, though he did not encourage reading or offer to buy a book.

A storm in the night was the means of getting Abe his first book. Josiah Crawford, a new settler, had a small library; while Abe worked for him, helping to build a house and to dig a well, he allowed Abe to borrow books. The evening Abe took home Ramsay's *Life of Washington* he read late, and then sleepily tucked the book into a chink between the logs by his bed. A rain blew up and soaked the book; Abe was dismayed when he saw its condition in the morning. Crawford would be furious—and rightly so. Abe took it to his employer immediately. The pages could be dried for reading, but the beauty of the volume was gone.

"Don't bring such a book to me!" Crawford shouted angrily. "You pull fodder in my cornfield for two days and keep the thing. I never want to see it again."

Abe pulled Crawford's fodder, and he was glad to own a book—but it was a long, long time before he had any pleasure in that one.

This reading, the friends he made, and the talk he heard gradually developed Abe Lincoln into a friendly youth who enjoyed new people, mastered good books, and could think on his feet. The years of his teens went by with nothing dramatic to mark them—yet he was growing steadily, as a tree grows season after season. Then in 1825 a new job was offered him, a job that brought him to the Ohio River.

Abe Lincoln was sixteen when James Taylor hired him to work on a farm by Posey's Landing. Taylor had a farm and a "Bank Store" on the riverbank where Anderson's Creek joined the Ohio River. Farmers and rivermen were his customers. When the job at Taylor's ended, Abe worked for other farmers, and then helped Taylor on his flatboat. They poled up and down the river collecting produce to sell. Abe liked this work; the steamboats, flatboats, and rafts filled with travelers fascinated him, and he earned six dollars a month.

In the summer of 1827, Abe built a scow for himself and did errands along the Indiana side of the Ohio. Sometimes he ferried travelers across Anderson's Creek when the water was high at the ford. He did not go across the Ohio because the Dill brothers, on the Kentucky side, had a ferry license for that work. His scow brought him many new experiences and the pleasure of meeting travelers.

One morning a stranger yelled at Abe when he was poling near the landing.

"Hi, *you!* See that steamboat comin'? Take me out to ketch 'er!" The man had stepped out on a great log and was waving his bandanna at the boat coming around the bend.

Abe saw that the Dills' ferry was tied up on the Kentucky bank; the steamboat was coming fast; and the captain signaled that he would stop in midstream, but would not turn to shore. "What ye waitin' fer?" the traveler complained. "I'll pay ye!"

Abe poled near. The man and his companion tossed bags aboard, and Abe put them on the steamboat.

"Here's yer pay!" As the paddles began to turn, the travelers tossed Abe two silver half-dollars.

Abe fingered the coins incredulously. A dollar! Three days of hog butchering would not earn that sum! After that he hung around the landing and made more money this way.

Alas! Unknown to Abe, the Dill brothers plotted to end his good fortune. They met Abe in mid river and pretended to be in trouble.

"Follow me, will ye, Abe?" John Dill begged. "I hain't sure I kin make it home." Abe followed them across; but the minute he was on land, John's brother leaped on him and accused him of stealing their trade. Abe made a quick thrust that knocked the man off and made the brothers change their minds about fighting him.

"We don't aim to fight," John said hastily. "In Kentuck' we go by the law. You come with us to Squire Pate, and he'll fix you."

Abe was willing; he didn't like a fight even when he won. They went to the squire's cabin nearby and the Dills swore out a warrant for Abe's arrest.

"Ready for the case, boys?" the squire asked. "Hain't much use waitin'."

They were ready. John Dill testified that he and his brother had the ferry license, but Abe Lincoln took passengers to board steamboats.

"The Kentucky line is 'low water' by the Indiana shore," Dill added.

The squire nodded. "Now state yer case," he told Abe. "They tell the truth," Abe granted. "But James Taylor says their license is to carry folks across. I only went to the middle of the river. I don't think I broke a law. Anyway, Squire, captains won't wait till a boat comes across to pick 'em up, and travelers hate to miss a boat."

"We'll see what the law says." Squire Pate took a book from his shelf, and as he turned pages the Dills observed that he was impressed with Abe's argument. "The law is plain," the squire announced. "You Dills have the right 'to set a person across,' but the law does not keep an unlicensed boatman from rowing passengers to midstream. The defendant is acquitted."

After the disappointed Dills left, Abe Lincoln lingered to talk with Squire Pate. "It's a wonder to me that you kin tell so quick what's right," he said.

"No wonder about it," the squire replied. "That book is *The Statutes of Kentucky*. Every man ought to know the statutes of his own state—'twould save him trouble. You come agin, son. You'll pick up a lot of law here. Might come handy some day fer you to know the law of the land."

Abe thanked the squire and went to his boat. As he crossed over to Taylor's those words, "the law of the land," echoed in his mind. They had a familiar sound. He thought of his mammy and their comfortable cabin in Kentucky; it was nearly eleven years since they had crossed this river, nearly nine, since she had died.

"Mammy al'ays wanted me to git eddicated," he remembered, and a plan shaped in his mind.

The next time he went to Turnham's he borrowed *The Revised Laws of Indiana*—a book he had seen on the office shelf. When he had mastered that, he borrowed a law book from Attorney Pitcher at Rockport. And whenever he could, he crossed the river to attend Squire Pate's monthly court.

But Abe said nothing at all of this at home. His father might not approve of his interest in Squire Pate and the law.

CHAPTER SIX

ABE'S HORIZON WIDENS

The law books and histories stirred Abe Lincoln's interest in his country's past and made him wonder what was happening now. Attorney Pitcher took the *Louisville Journal,* and William Jones—the storekeeper from Vincennes—subscribed for his home-town paper, the *Western Sun.* Abe read these newspapers and names in the news—Jackson, Clay, Calhoun, Hayne, Webster—came alive to him and were not just words on a page.

Daniel Webster.

Most of his neighbors had been so busy with their own affairs that they rarely thought of the world beyond Pigeon Creek. But after they were settled, that gradually changed—though unfortunately few men could read enough to enjoy a newspaper. Men got into the habit of lingering at Jones's store, where Abe Lincoln sold goods and then read the *Sun* aloud. Jones's crossroads store was only one of hundreds of places where people were getting news in the late 1820s. Journeymen printers set up presses in towns in the Middle West. They printed bits of local news and long speeches brought to them by postrider or by boat. Discussions on subjects formerly argued only in Congress were carried on in a thousand corner stores.

During this same time, while he was still "hiring out," Abe Lincoln walked hundreds of miles—to Gentry's, to Jones's, sixteen miles southeast to Taylor's, eighteen miles southwest to Rockport, and to farms in between. His father seldom let him use a horse unless he was returning the same day. Somewhere Abe had picked up a sick dog—left, perhaps, by a family traveling west—and after he had nursed the mongrel back to health, the dog followed him devotedly. Otherwise Abe usually walked alone. But he found that walking went well with reading; it gave him time to think. Speeches needed "thinking over," if a youth was to understand them. As he mulled over each one, Abe Lincoln discovered that four or five subjects were the most discussed—orators called these subjects "issues"; but really they were questions that American people were trying to decide.

Abe listened as men in the store had long discussions about a national bank. Some thought it was better for each state to print its own money. They quarreled about the tariff—a tax on merchandise brought into the country. Some thought it was a good thing and some were against it.

But Abe's neighbors did not argue about improving roads and building canals, because they knew that Indiana needed both. They didn't care much who paid for the work just so it was done soon. They didn't care, either, whether families moving west had to pay for land or could get it free; as for slavery, Indiana was a nonslave state. But Abe found many speeches on those matters, and knew people somewhere were thinking about each one.

In the summer of 1828 southern Indianans got excited about politics and the national election. Villages held rallies; speakers toured on horseback and talked to large groups. Thomas Lincoln and Dennis Hanks were for Andrew Jackson. His war record, his humble Carolina birth, and his many fine qualities inspired followers. Pitcher and others Abe admired were for John Quincy Adams, the man Clay was working for. They called themselves "Whigs"—a word borrowed from England years earlier.

"Who you fer?" Abe was often asked. He grinned—and said nothing. He couldn't vote yet, and he worked for many of the Jackson men—what good would it do to take sides?

Toward the end of the campaign Abe was offered work that would take him far from home. Mr. Gentry planned to sell his autumn produce in New Orleans and needed a helper for his son Allen, who was to take the trip.

"Get Abe Lincoln to go with me," Allen begged his father. "He is strong and handy and we work well together."

So Gentry offered Abe the work and he accepted. Allen and Abe were to build the flatboat at Gentry's Landing below the bluff at Rockport, load the produce, and take it to New Orleans. Gentry agreed to pay eight dollars a month and his return passage by steamboat; so Thomas Lincoln was willing for Abe to go. The trip would be an adventure; it would be hard work and dangerous at times, too, for pirates often raided a well-stocked boat, snags and rapids made navigation hard, and thieves might sneak aboard at night. Abe knew that there was much more to a river trip than merely floating downstream!

A few weeks after Andrew Jackson was elected president in November, the boat was finished and loaded with corn, flour, potatoes, bacon, and hams. Townspeople came to the landing to wish the boys luck, and Allen's wife (the Ann Roby of Abe's spelling-match days) waved from the top of the bluff as their boat swung out into the current.

Traveling was lonesome, for there were few boats at this season; but the weather was good, and solitude had advantages. The pirates' hideout at Cave-in-Rock seemed deserted when they passed it.

The last night of the voyage they tied up at a dock to get some sleep. The treacherous current of that day's course had exhausted them. The night was dark, the place quiet, and they slept heavily.

A rough hand on his shoulder awakened Abe. His training through years of sleeping in the forest had taught him to waken instantly.

"Allen!" he yelled. "Allen! Watch out!" As he shouted, Abe twisted free and flung the intruder head over heels into the river. His long arms flailed around in the darkness; he caught two more thieves and tossed them into the water. By then, Allen was up and fighting. They grabbed clubs, which they kept handy, and chased four men to shore.

"We've got to push off," Abe whispered, as he and Allen climbed back into the boat.

"In the dark?" Allen objected. "You know how the current is, Abe."

"I know they're likely to fetch a gang back with 'em," Abe retorted, "and next time they wouldn't count on us being asleep. They didn't relish gittin' licked—you saw that."

Abe cast off and took the place at the wide sweep. Only then he noticed that he had a deep cut above his right ear. He bound it up the best he could, but he carried the scar all his life.

The next day they came to New Orleans, and Abe was free to explore the city while Allen traded the flatboat and its cargo for cotton, tobacco, and sugar which would be shipped to Rockport by steamboat. The city seemed to Abe like a place in *The Arabian Nights*. He stood before the cathedral with its tall spires, strolled on sidewalks above the mud, stared at gaily tinted houses and the balconies with their lacy wrought-iron grillwork. He smelled new fruits and the horrid stench of the slave market; heard a dozen new tongues—French, Spanish, Italian—and the songs of sailors on ships at the wharves. New Orleans was overwhelming; he was almost glad when it was time to leave. On the journey home he saw still more sights from the steamboat's high deck—sights they had missed when the low flatboat floated south.

When at last he arrived home, Abe found that his father was disturbed and restless. John Hanks, the son of that carpenter, Joseph Hanks, who had taught Thomas his trade, had visited the Lincolns while Abe was away. John Hanks now lived in Illinois and had excited his host by tales of that state.

"John says they's acres of land without trees in Illinois," Thomas Lincoln told Abe. "He says a man needn't chop down a forest to grow his bit of corn. Jest break the prairie grass an' plant." He looked at Abe wondering how the youth would take this news.

"I heard talk about prairie land on the steamboat," Abe told his father.

"Maybe John's tales were true!" Lincoln exclaimed incredulously.

"I'm glad you're home, Abe," Mrs. Lincoln said. "Your pappy is restless and talks of moving."

"I'm sick of trees and no water handy," Lincoln complained. But he did nothing about a move. Abe continued to work for hire through the summer of 1829.

In the autumn travelers brought rumors of "milk sickness." All who remembered the epidemic of 1818 were frightened.

"That settles it," Thomas Lincoln decided. "We'll git out." He called the family together and told them they were moving to Illinois.

His family was very different now from that of ten years before when the three Johnston and two Lincoln children had crowded their cabin. Death and marriages had altered the group. Elizabeth Johnston and Dennis's Hanks had married and now had three children. Young Sarah Lincoln had married a neighbor and had died two years later. Matilda Johnston had married Levi Hall, a relative of Dennis's and they had two children. John Johnston was a lad of fifteen, and Abe Lincoln a tall youth nearing twenty-one.

"Me an' Elizabeth'll go with ye," Dennis said quickly. "It'll give our children a better chanct."

"Me an' Tilly'll go," Levi Hall agreed. The young people had talked it over many an evening and had decided. Abe's opinion wasn't asked. He had to go with his father the same as a fourteen-year-old.

Thomas Lincoln sold his land to James Gentry and traded his stock for four oxen. Working together the men built two wagons big enough to carry all their household goods. The cabins were buzzing with activity all winter; Thomas Lincoln was like a new man, excited about starting over in a new place. Word was sent to John Hanks to select land with plenty of water.

Preparations were going well when on a January morning Abe went to Jones's store to get some nails. He found that a copy of the *Sun* had come, and he read a speech Senator Hayne of South Carolina had made about the tariff and state's rights. South Carolina planters were having a poor market for their cotton, and Hayne said that the tariff hurt their business. A state should have the right, he said, to manage its own affairs. South Carolina had threatened to leave the Union.

A few days later Abe read Daniel Webster's brilliant reply to Hayne. Webster said that the power of the federal government was given to it by the states and all should support the Constitution. If any change was needed it should be done by law, not by threats of seceding that might lead to a civil war. Webster pleaded for unity and patience.

"You read that agin, Abe," Jones said; so Abe reread the final paragraph:

> *While the Union lasts we have high prospects spread out before us, for us and for our children—liberty first and Union afterward (says Hayne)—I speak another sentiment dear to every American heart—Liberty AND Union, now and forever.*

Men in the store approved those sentiments, and Abe walked home through the snow with the stirring words echoing in his head.

Soon after this, about the first of March, 1830, the Lincoln clan left Pigeon Creek for Illinois. The wagons were piled high with spinning wheels, chests, looms, blankets, chairs, frying pans, and scores of household things. Children and women rode; men walked ahead and took turns guiding the oxen. Abe's dog trotted alongside him, and over his shoulder Abe carried a sack filled with needles, pins, and buttons which he hoped to sell along the way. (He had got these things from Jones in payment for doing chores.) When a cabin was sighted, Abe would run ahead and with his persuasive manner he usually sold something. He made a good profit on this first business venture.

Before they crossed the Wabash River at Vincennes, Abe saw the press that printed the *Sun*. He was entranced with the noise and rhythmic movement of the machine. It seemed like a miracle!

A few miles after Vincennes, floating ice in a creek jammed the wagon wheels; the boys had to wade in and heave to get them moving. When the wagon reached the bank, Abe turned to take his boots from Tilly and spied his dog whining on the far side.

"I told ye to keep my dog up top when we crossed," he called to the children. "We have to go back, Pappy, an' git my dog."

"Go back? Not me!" Lincoln retorted. "What's a dog? You come on!" The wagons continued west.

Abe looked despairingly at his dog. The water was ice-cold; his feet were numb. Yet that dog had such confidence Abe couldn't disappoint him.

"Jest give me time, Old Fellow," he said quietly. "I'm comin'!"

He dropped his boots, waded across, picked up the dog, and splashed back through the ice. The dog licked his face gratefully, and Abe grinned at him.

"You stay on the wagon, next creek we come to," he advised as he worried his numb feet into wet boots. But his tone was kind; the dog understood.

In this way Abe Lincoln, soon after his twenty-first birthday, came into the prairie state called Illinois.

CHAPTER SEVEN

RUTLEDGE DAM

Thomas Lincoln liked the piece of land selected for them in central Illinois; it was timberland along the Sangamon River, with level prairie beyond. Lincoln, Hall, and Dennis chose portions of land, and helped each other build cabins. Abe and his father then plowed, fenced, and planted ten acres of corn. Thomas Lincoln went at this work briskly, confident that his fortunes had improved.

Even before his work was finished Abe Lincoln was offered a job. Illinois was rapidly being settled; more than one hundred thousand people had

La Grange Lock and Dam on the Illinois River in Versailles, Illinois.

moved into the state between 1820 and 1830. Every family had to build a home, and farmers needed help in plowing and fencing. As soon as he could be spared at home, Abe began hiring out. Usually he boarded where he worked and returned between jobs to give his father a lift.

Now that he had passed his twenty-first birthday, he could keep his earnings. Often he worked for clothing instead of for money. He split four hundred rails for each yard of homespun jeans-cloth, and then more rails when the farmer's wife made the cloth into breeches. He gained a reputation for strength and speed, and one employer recommended him to another.

"Hire that tall feller," a newcomer was advised. "He splits rails like a giant."

"Jest give that Abe Lincoln some folks to watch him and he'll split rails fit ter kill," another remarked. But some were more observing.

"That Abe, he works till he gits men watchin' and then he rests his ax and tells a tale," a man who had hired Abe explained. "But ye kaint help but like his yarns. Hit haint *what* he tells, hit's his way of talkin'. Yesterday I laughed till my sides ached—don' know what *at!* Jest him, I reckon."

Abe Lincoln made droll tales of his adventures in Indiana forests, on the Ohio River, and in New Orleans—and told them with zest and a grin.

But by late summer the Lincoln family fortunes took a turn for the worse. "Chills and fever" made much illness in central Illinois, and the following winter a terrible snowstorm killed stock and ruined stored crops. Snow was five feet deep on the prairie, and drifts buried entire cabins. The temperature was twenty degrees below zero, the coldest ever remembered. Thomas Lincoln was very ill and Abe had to stay home and help out, though he had taken on a big job for the winter.

Major Warnick, who had a farm across the Sangamon, had hired Abe to split three thousand rails. Abe had planned to live at home and tend stock for his board. He had built a canoe for going back and forth to work. As soon as his father recovered, Abe pushed across the swollen river to Warnick's. Ice floes overturned his boat in midstream, and he barely got it and himself to shore. When he reached the farmhouse his feet were numb.

"Abe Lincoln! You've frozen your feet!" Mrs. Warnick exclaimed when she opened the door. "You'll be lucky if you save them!" She rubbed his feet with snow, dressed them with ointment she had made, and bandaged them. Soon the misery of returning circulation was almost more than Abe could endure.

For two weeks Abe suffered agony while his feet healed. The Warnicks were kind, but he was lonely. He missed old friends and the talk at Jones's store. At night he sat for hours— his back propped against an overturned chair, his feet itching and throbbing—and wondered what to do with his life.

"Here I am," he mused, "soon twenty-two years old; and since I started drappin' pumpkin seeds fer Pappy I've farmed enough to last me a lifetime—but what else kin I do? I've seen no books around here—met no lawyers. Likely they's plenty of both in Illinois, but how kin I find 'em? I reckon I kaint do anything but hire out."

One such night he recalled an event of the previous summer. A stranger had happened by while several men were working, Abe among them. The man had made a political speech; when he finished, John Hanks spoke up.

"My partner here kin talk better'n him," John had boasted. "Show 'em, Abe."

Abe promptly laid aside his ax, mounted a stump, and made a talk about improving the channel of the Sangamon River. The men had applauded his words: they understood his ideas better than the stranger's vague generalities.

"I liked makin' that speech," Abe remembered now. "I like to talk. But a feller kaint earn a livin' talkin'—not as I ever heard of."

In the morning he realized that his first task was to split rails. He must do more than the three thousand because he owed Warnick for two weeks' board.

Abe was still splitting rails when a new man named Denton Offutt came to Warnick's. Offutt was well dressed in a flashy style; he was a loud talker, full of ideas and grand plans. He offered Abe a job, taking produce to New Orleans; and Abe accepted for himself and for his stepbrother, seventeen-year-old John Johnston.

"You boys meet me and John Hanks at Portland Landing soon as the ice goes out," Offutt ordered. (This place was the point on the Sangamon nearest to the town of Springfield.) "I'll have a boat and cargo there ready for the trip. You'll make good pay." And he swaggered away.

When Abe had finished Warnick's rails, he and young Johnston hollowed out a cottonwood log and floated down to

Portland Landing. Offutt was not there. So they walked the six miles to Springfield, where they found him in a tavern. He had no flatboat and no cargo.

Abe and John hated to give up their bright prospects, so they offered to build a boat. Offutt promised to pay them twelve dollars a month and told them to build it on the Sangamon. He hired John Hanks to help them.

Abe Lincoln elected himself cook at their camp and so managed to avoid some hard work at mealtimes. Weather was warmer now. Cardinals and catbirds darted through the pussy willows; prairie chickens cackled among the buttercups and violets. Abe snagged game and cooked corndodgers, which went well with the honey he discovered in a stump. With twelve dollars a month for each, the boys didn't rush the work. Word of their boat got around and quite a crowd gathered for the launching. Whigs and Democrats came and made political speeches, and a juggler turned up to amuse the crowd.

"Any feller got a hat I kin use?" he asked in the middle of his performance.

"Take Abe Lincoln's!" a youngster shouted. The boy had admired the low-crowned, broad-rimmed hat Abe was wearing. (The coonskin cap with dangling tail had been discarded as the weather warmed.)

Abe hesitated but, when urged, passed up his precious headgear. The magician cooked two eggs in it and returned it with a flourish.

"You see, ye got yer hat back," he twitted.

"My hesitation, sir, was out of respect for your eggs, not for my hat," Abe explained with great dignity. The crowd roared.

The next day the builders loaded the flatboat with cargo Offutt had purchased—sacks of corn, barrels of bacon and hams, and live hogs. At the last minute John Hanks could not take the whole trip. But Offutt decided they could manage without him and soon they were rounding the bend of the river and approaching the town of New Salem.

Here, two years earlier, James Rutledge and his nephew John Camron had built a strong dam with wooden crates filled with a thousand loads of gravel. They had also built a two-story gristmill and sawmill, and developed a prosperous business. On the bluff above Rutledge Dam was the little village of New Salem. Already, in this spring of 1831, it was the size of Chicago, a small village near Fort Dearborn on Lake Michigan. Settlers were boasting that before long New Salem would grow to be a big city.

The crew of the flatboat were looking at the bluff when the boat hit that dam with a bang. The prow tilted high, the stern sank and filled with water. Hogs squealed. Barrels rolled. Sacks of corn tumbled helter-skelter. The pandemonium brought villagers to stare at the scene. Rutledge and Camron stopped the mill.

"Get off that dam!" Rutledge shouted. Camron shook his fist threateningly.

Small boys slid down the hillside while older youths came out in small boats to lend a hand. Abe pushed up his breeches, waded in, and lifted squealing hogs onto these boats. The flatboat didn't move, though the load was lightened. Offutt was not in sight, so Abe followed his own hunch.

"Could I borry an auger?" he asked the crowd.

"Henry Onstot, the cooper, has one," a mannerly voice answered. Abe saw that the speaker was a dignified gentleman of medium height who, unlike the others who were dressed in homespun, wore a neat black suit and a white shirt. Beside him was a golden-haired girl who held a bit of sewing in her hands.

Abe stared—but this was not the time to look at fashions or pretty girls. Those hogs were squealing! A youngster fetched the auger; Abe splashed back to the flatboat and went to work at the prow.

"He's boring a hole!" a boy shouted.

"An' hit stickin' in the air!" another scoffed.

Abe didn't glance toward shore. A hole made, he leaped onto the flatboat and yelled to John Johnston.

"Roll 'em forward!" he said as he began moving barrels. John sprang to help. When six barrels had been moved forward the prow tipped downward a few inches.

"That's the idear!" the crowd now approved. "Move 'em all." Soon the prow sank—lower and slowly lower. Water drained forward and out through the hole as the boat fell forward— and over the dam—while Abe thrust a plug into the hole.

"I never thought they'd get it over," Camron was saying as Abe splashed by to return the auger and reload the hogs. Offutt returned when the work was done and they pushed off.

"Mighty nice little place, that New Salem," Offutt announced agreeably, as they floated away, "right on the road between Springfield and Monmouth. Did you boys notice the good level land on the bluff? A fine site for a town."

Abe grinned. Offutt knew he had not been sight-seeing.

"They've got a tavern, a cooper shop, and two or three stores. I hear that on Saturdays fifty horses are tied up on that hill, the men waiting a turn at the mill. They ought to have more stores for such a town. I bought a lot and paid ten dollars to have my store built. I wasn't idling while you got us over the dam, Abe.

"How'd you like to clerk in my store when we git back from New Orleans?"

"I'd like hit right well," Abe admitted.

They floated to the Illinois River, to the Mississippi, and down to New Orleans. While Offutt sold his cargo and the boat, Abe revisited the city. He saw a slave girl on the auction block—a sight that stayed with him always, and marred his pleasure in the city. Soon they traveled north by steamer to St. Louis. Offutt hired young John to help him there as he assembled goods for the new store. Abe walked the hundred miles home; as he followed the prairie trail, he wondered how he would find his family. His father had vowed he would move.

Thomas Lincoln had kept his word; he had bought land in Coles County, about fifty miles to the southeast. Abe helped them move, build a good cabin, plant and fence a field. Then he said good-by to his parents and left for New Salem.

As Abe tramped west over the prairie, he thought with pleasure of his new job. He was through with hiring out to farmers, through with being only a son in the house of a man who thought that reading was a waste of time. He stayed overnight at John Hanks's house and pushed off the next morning in the canoe he'd had the year before. The rest of his journey would be easy—just floating down the Sangamon.

Hot July sun beat down while Abe thought over his life and his prospects. In New Salem he might find books. Offutt had said that the well-dressed gentleman was a schoolmaster and that the townfolk were fine people. The Illinois men Abe had met had faith in the future of the country and in the prospects of the common man. "An American can do anything!" was a phrase heard daily.

Anything? If he had the choosing, what would he be, Abe wondered, and was surprised to find the answer, ready in his mind. "I'd be a lawyer!" He thought of Attorney Pitcher and Squire Pate, and suddenly a picture flashed before his mind—a remembered scene, vivid as a man recalls a scene of early childhood. He saw himself and Sarah sitting on a woodpile and a man passing by. He seemed to hear his mammy's voice saying, "That man's a lawyer. He knows the law of the land."

As though her hand was on his shoulder, Abe Lincoln felt assured of his destiny. His mammy would have said that God was guiding him.

His faith in himself was strengthened. He knew no more than before what he would do and how he would do it. But now he knew that there was a place in the world for him and that he was going to it.

CHAPTER EIGHT

THE CLARY GROVE BOYS

After these pleasant daydreams it was a severe blow to find that Offutt's store was not built. Abe Lincoln turned from the vacant lot on the bluff and looked down at his canoe, tied to a tree. Perhaps he should go back to John Hanks and find work there? But the feeling that his destiny was here persisted. He walked west on the road through New Salem.

A group of men were standing in front of a cabin; as he came near Abe surmised that they were holding an election. In frontier villages where

Bare-fisted boxers pose.

few men could read and write, a voter stated his choice to clerks, who marked the vote on tally sheets. Abe stepped near enough to glance at those sheets— perhaps he could recognize some name Offutt had mentioned. The men stared at the stranger, and one spoke to him.

"I see you can read," this villager remarked; "can you write?" Abe recognized him as the well-dressed man who had offered the auger the day the flatboat hit the dam. "I kin make a few hen tracks," Lincoln acknowledged, smiling.

"Then will you help us out? I am Mentor Graham, the village schoolmaster. Abram Bergen, the other clerk, had to leave though the election is not quite over. We shall be grateful for your help."

"I kin try," Lincoln said. "I'm Abe Lincoln, come to work for Denton Offutt." Before he had time to say more, two men stepped forward to vote and Abe slipped into Bergen's place by the table.

The voting soon ended, but men lingered around the table to hear the results and to talk politics. Abe was interested and joined in their discussion. He quoted speeches of Henry Clay and Daniel Webster and expressed opinions about temperance, the need for good roads, and about the Federal government. Graham was astonished. The stranger's clothing was shabby and his language crude, yet he had considerable knowledge of public affairs. Graham invited Abe to supper, and he had his eighteen-year-old cousin Billy Greene come with them.

During the meal Lincoln learned that Graham was from Kentucky and knew friends of Thomas Lincoln and that he had faith in the future of New Salem.

"I believe this village will grow to be a city," Graham said. "We are on a good river, and already we have a thriving mill business."

"I think I have the chanct fer a right smart shake with Offutt," Lincoln told him.

Graham approved the ambition but winced at the language. An idea for helping his visitor occurred to him.

"We have a debating society here," he said. "We meet weekly and discuss current questions. I shall be glad to take you with me next week, and if you wish, I shall propose you for membership."

"I thank you kindly, sir!" Lincoln's quick acceptance showed Graham that the idea of debate was pleasing.

Abe lingered till late that evening and from Graham learned a good deal about the villagers. Many—like the miller Rutledge, of South Carolina—had brought large families when they came to Illinois; his daughter Ann was the golden-haired girl Abe had seen in the spring. Rutledge had a tavern, too, and was an influential man in the village. Others were single men, like John McNeil who came to New Salem from the East. These unmarried men had come west to make fame and fortune. Some of them were well educated and had small libraries in their log cabins. Dr. Allen was a graduate of Dartmouth College; Jack Kelso was a kind of philosopher and a student of Shakespeare and Burns. Others in the neighborhood were a rough frontier sort like John Clary and his clan from Tennessee. Graham's information pleased Abe Lincoln. He went home with Billy Greene and for a while boarded with the Greenes.

Offutt arrived a few days later, bringing merchandise. Abe and Offutt built a cabin and arranged the stock of calico, sugar, salt, coffee, tea, bonnets, and hardware on the new shelves—and the store opened for business.

Abe Lincoln found that he liked storekeeping in Illinois even better than in Indiana. On Saturdays he had to work steadily, but he enjoyed the talk of men who stayed around after their buying was finished. On other days he had hours for reading—and he didn't have to walk miles to borrow books. He made friends with Jack Kelso; and when he found that Mrs. Kelso took in boarders because Jack liked fishing and reading better than earning, he moved to their home.

In the evenings he discussed poetry and drama with Jack and recited long passages that he had memorized. The rhythms of this literature became fixed in his mind along with Bible chapters he had learned earlier.

Soon after the store opened Offutt grew restless and looked around for something new.

"I'm thinking of buying another store," he boasted, "or maybe a mill or a tavern."

"You've got a store a'ready," Onstot the cooper reminded him. Onstot was a steady man.

"One store don't tie *me* up!" Offutt retorted. "I may buy a steamboat and run a line up here from Cincinnati—that would boom this town!" Men thought him a marvel.

"Anyhow, this store don't worry me," Offutt continued, enjoying his own talk. "I've got the best clerk a man could have—that Abe Lincoln! He can outrun, outfight, outthrow any man in Sangamon County!" He eyed the crowd daringly.

"Is that so!" Bill Clary exclaimed scornfully. "You have to prove that!"

Young Clary was one of John Clary's sons; they had a farm three miles southwest of town. The Clarys and their relatives had gathered around them quite a group of strapping fellows who called themselves "Clary Grove Boys." They were honest men, but rough and quarrelsome, and they respected nothing but physical strength. Jack Armstrong, their leader at the moment, had earned his place by hard hitting. And now Offutt boasted about a new man. The boys resented it.

Clary bet Offutt that Jack Armstrong could lick Abe Lincoln, and a match was arranged for the next Saturday afternoon. Offutt always had an eye for business; a fight would draw men to his store.

After the plans were made, Abe was told; but he did not object.

Saturday the opponents faced each other in a ring marked near the store. Jack was short but powerfully built and confident; Abe was tall and lean. Jack drew in blusteringly, but Abe's long arms held him off so easily that Jack's temper flared. He jammed his right foot on Abe's instep.

The pain infuriated Abe. He grabbed Jack by the back of the neck, held him high, shook him like a dishrag, and tossed him aside. The Clary Grove boys stared, speechless. Was this their bold leader—this man tossed into the dust? They sprang at Abe angrily.

"I'll fight every man of you—one at a time," Abe yelled as he backed against the store wall. "Who's first?"

No one moved.

Jack Armstrong stirred, feebly. The crowd watched as he crawled to his feet, tottered over to Abe, and shook the winner's hand.

"He won, fair enough," the fallen leader announced. The gang eyed Abe respectfully. They saw a tall man of some hundred and eighty pounds with unruly black hair, keen eyes, and a long, thin face that could smile all over. Suddenly Bill Clary recalled that Abe was the youth who had so cleverly got the flatboat over Rutledge Dam.

"Smart as a whip, he is, too," Clary announced. He put out his hand—and Abe Lincoln was accepted as leader.

Winning this match so soon after he came to New Salem was a major event in Abraham Lincoln's life. Those Clary Grove boys ruled the community; now he was their leader. As they came to know him they discovered some strange facts: he did not smoke, chew, or drink—and he had a passion for reading. Usually they called such a man a "sissy," but a fighter like Abe was no sissy; so they simply agreed that he "had notions." He was more honest than a man need be, they thought, when he walked miles to return a few pennies a farmer's wife had overpaid at the store; and he was strict about fair play.

On the first wave of his popularity he was chosen as a "second" in a fight. The other second, a bantam-sized youth, challenged Abe.

"Sure, I'll fight ye," Abe agreed cheerfully. "You chalk up on me where your head comes and that much of me will fight you." The crowd roared at the challenger's astonishment, and no more was said about that fight.

But in spite of the clerk's popularity, Offutt's store failed early in 1832 and Abe was again out of work. Since he had some money saved and could pay his board, he decided to use the time for reading and wait for something to turn up.

Schoolmaster Graham often invited Abe over in the evenings and they talked about books. But Abe's pioneer talk fretted him.

"Your language is understood here," Graham said, "even when you debate. But if you want a larger audience you must improve your vocabulary. Train yourself to say 'I am not' instead of 'I haint.' Remember the word is 'for' and not 'fer.' And if you ever wish to write, Abe, you must study grammar."

Abe liked that idea. "Where could I get a grammar?" he asked.

"I can loan you my book in the evenings," Graham said. "But I need it at school during the day." Then he pondered a minute.

"My old friend Vance has a copy of Kirkham's *Grammar*, but he lives eight miles from here, in the country."

"Eight miles is no distance!" Abe laughed, "I thank you for the suggestion."

He studied Graham's copy that evening and the next morning tramped out to borrow from Vance. This Kirkham's *Grammar* was a difficult book, but Abe went at it with determination. Section by section he memorized that volume. Abe did more than memorize, he got the meaning of each rule.

His speech improved, and before long he excelled his teacher in the written expression of his thought.

Lincoln always felt handicapped by what he called "his lack of education." In this he made the common mistake of thinking that going to school was "education." In all, he had less than twelve months in schools in Kentucky and Indiana; but in those schools he acquired the basic tools for learning—reading, writing, and simple arithmetic. Afterward he used those tools to learn whatever he needed to know for the work he chose to do. His speeches, writings, and lifework prove that he was well educated, and that anyone who is willing to work and can borrow books can educate himself.

Perhaps about the time of Abe's twenty-third birthday, someone proposed that he try for election as state representative from Sangamon County. Friends urged him to campaign, and he turned over in his mind a plan of action.

At that time a candidate for the Legislature wrote out his statement of principles in the form of a letter which was then printed in a newspaper or on handbills. Voters were "for" this man or that one, instead of for a party and its platform. Andrew Jackson was President and would run for re-election in the fall; most pioneer voters were "Jackson men." Abe Lincoln was for Clay. But national issues made little difference when voters elected their state representatives. They would vote for a man they knew and who would help pass laws that would improve Sangamon County conditions.

Lincoln's letter was a clear statement of his beliefs on subjects important to local voters. The Springfield paper, the *Sangamo Journal*, printed it on March 9, 1832.

After introducing himself, Lincoln wrote about Sangamon County's chief need—transportation for getting produce to markets.

Lincoln's practical suggestion was that the Sangamon River be straightened and deepened, work which he thought would cost less than railroads. He wrote next about fair rates of interest (a big problem for new settlers who must borrow capital), and then about the need for better schools. He ended with a paragraph that was very revealing about himself:

> *Every man is said to have his peculiar ambition. Whether it be true or not, I can say for one that I have no other so great as that of being truly esteemed of my fellow men, by rendering myself worthy of their esteem. How far I shall succeed in gratifying this ambition, is yet to be developed.*
>
> *I am young and unknown to many of you. I was born and have ever remained in the most humble walks of life. I have no wealthy or popular relations to recommend me. My case is thrown exclusively upon the independent voters of this county, and if elected they will have conferred a favor upon me, for which I shall be unremitting in my labors to compensate. But if the good people in their wisdom shall see fit to keep me in the back ground, I have been too familiar with disappointments to be very much chagrined.*

With this statement back of him, Lincoln planned to get out and campaign for election.

CHAPTER NINE

TWICE A CANDIDATE

Abe Lincoln liked the appearance of his letter in the newspaper. But before he got his campaign under way, new and exciting news was brought to New Salem by a traveler from Beardstown, thirty miles to the west.

A mill owner, Vincent Bogue of Portland Landing, was coming up the Sangamon in a chartered steamer, the *Talisman*, with goods from Cincinnati. Now with New Salem on a commercial waterway, the long-hoped-for boom would come!

Soon Bogue and his steamboat arrived at Beardstown. He sent messengers to New Salem

Chicago in 1820.

for workers. They were to meet his steamer at the mouth of the *Sangamon* and lop off overhanging branches that might harm the steamer's paint. Abe Lincoln was hired as one of this gang.

When the *Talisman* steamed past New Salem, the bluff was packed with villagers eager to see the gleaming white and gold boat and to cheer as her twin stacks sent smoke drifting over the prairie. Many people went to share in a great celebration.

On April 5, 1832, Springfield's newspaper, the *Sangamo Journal*, printed an account of this event and even a "poem" written in honor of the occasion. People quoted favorite lines:

> *If Jason who the golden fleece*
> *Sailed for many years from Greece*
> *To such a height of fame did get*
> *The Argonaut's remembered yet*
> *Then what a debt of fame we owe*
> *To him who on our Sangamo*
> *First launched the steamer's daring prow.*
> *What think ye, laddie, isn't it grand*
> *To see a steamer touch our strand?*

The cargo sold at a profit and the captain was entertained till someone noticed that the high water was gone. If he wanted to go back to Ohio, the captain had better go while he could still float his boat!

Bogue engaged Rowan Herndon and Abe Lincoln to help him steam down river and all was well till they came to the Rutledge Dam. No clever trick could get this big steamer over!

"We'll have to remove part of your dam," Herndon yelled.

"Ye ain't allowed to touch it," Rutledge shouted back.

"You daren't obstruct a navigable river," Abe Lincoln announced firmly. Rutledge was silenced, for he too, knew the law. He fumed while Herndon and Lincoln laboriously removed part of the dam, got the steamer over, and made the repairs required by law.

New Salem people watched sadly. Such difficulty, early in the season, showed that the Sangamon could not be depended on. The boom was over. That inglorious retreat of the *Talisman* marked the end of New Salem's hopes of becoming a great city.

Lincoln walked back to the village expecting to find his friends discouraged. Instead they were excited about a war and the governor's call for volunteers to settle a dispute with the Indians.

Abe Lincoln and about twenty-five others from New Salem enlisted and went to Richland to enter the service. Lincoln was gratified when the company selected him captain. This honor was more than leadership of a gang; it was an election that gave him a responsible job for his country.

He did his best to train his men for battle, but they had no chance to show their bravery. After the month ended, many went home. Lincoln decided to re-enlist. This time he was a private among strangers, and again he had no chance to fight; for the Sac Chief, Black Hawk, was taken prisoner and his people driven across the Mississippi. Soon Abe's company was mustered out in southern Wisconsin, and men from Sangamon County walked home together.

On this journey Abe Lincoln became acquainted with John A. Stuart, a young attorney from Springfield. Stuart was a well-educated Kentucky aristocrat who had come to Illinois in 1828. He was a Whig and two years older than Lincoln; he practiced law in Springfield, had influence in the county, and was running for election to the State Legislature, as Lincoln was. Stuart liked Abe and encouraged him to study law and to run for the state office. As they tramped south the two men became friends, and Abe discovered that Stuart had what Abe wanted most—law books which he was willing to lend to a new friend.

The Black Hawk War was a minor event in national history but a major factor in Lincoln's development. It brought him his first election, the captaincy, and introduced him to a man competent and willing to help him study law. His feeling that destiny sent him to New Salem had been right; in the year that he had lived there, he had attained leadership in his community, improved his education, and had found a lawyer friend who would help him.

His next step was to start his campaign. Election day was less than two weeks away.

Since the time was so short, Abe decided to make a direct appeal to the voters. At harvest time men got together for the auction of livestock, for cornhusking, and for other seasonal work; and they liked some political talk when the job was done. Lincoln's first chance to speak came at an auction nearby.

Chicago in 1820.

He arrived early, dressed in his best—a coat of mixed-jeans, cut claw-hammer fashion (with sleeves and coattails too short), tow-and-flax pantaloons, and a straw hat without a band. He visited with the men and made a campaign speech. His statement of principles got attention, and his backwoods tales delighted them. A favorite yarn was about a preacher who during a long sermon felt a lizard crawling up inside his breeches. Abe Lincoln's gifted mimicry as he acted out the preacher's frantic misery had the men rocking with laughter.

Encouraged by this modest success, Lincoln tramped from place to place around New Salem. Just before election day he went to Springfield for a meeting where all candidates spoke.

Lincoln lost the election; he stood eighth among the thirteen who contested. John Stuart was among the fortunate four who were elected. But, though he lost, Lincoln had profited by trying. He had learned to speak in public, he had made many friends, and—at the Springfield meeting—he had become acquainted with Stephen T. Logan, a prominent attorney. Like Stuart, Logan was a Whig from Kentucky. He was already considered one of the best lawyers in the state. Now Abe had two lawyer friends in Springfield.

"I didn't do badly," Abe Lincoln consoled himself. "If I had had more time I might have won." He was proud that all but seven of the New Salem men had voted for him.

The campaign over, there was the matter of earning a living. Abe called on James Herndon, who with his brother Rowan had a store in New Salem, and asked for a job as a clerk.

"Me need a clerk?" Herndon growled. "Business is so

bad that I'm more likely to sell out than to hire! This town has been dead since the steamboat line busted. But you're welcome to live here, Abe, till you get settled."

Soon James Herndon did sell out his half interest to a William Berry and Rowan sold his half to Lincoln, taking Abe's promise in payment. So Lincoln, to his amazement, found himself a penniless half owner of a store under the name of the Lincoln-Berry Store. Of course there was a debt of several hundred dollars but that did not worry Lincoln— nor Herndon either, for he knew Abe was honest.

During the next few months (in late 1832 and early 1833) Lincoln had a comfortable life. He roomed back of the store, and had time to read and to enjoy his neighbors. The Rutledge tavern was just across the way. Ann often came in to buy for the family, and they talked about books and their ambitions. On Saturdays the store was full of customers.

During this time Abe Lincoln often went to Springfield to borrow books from Stuart or Logan and to talk with them about the books he returned. On one trip he chanced to hear of an auction in town. He strolled over, arriving as a copy of Blackstone's *Commentaries* (a basic law book) was put up for sale. He bought it and stumbled all the way home as he tried to read and walk across the prairie!

But alas! Bill Berry's carelessness and Lincoln's devotion to reading did not help business. Women who came to buy found Bill asleep and Abe deep in Thomas Paine's *Age of Reason*, good-humored enough but not much interested in matching thread or buttons. Few shared the owner's surprise when the store failed. Soon after his twenty-fourth birthday Lincoln was jobless again and in debt. A few months later Berry died, leaving the whole sum for Abe to pay.

At that time, most men in such a situation simply left town and started over in a new place. But Abe Lincoln had a firm faith in himself and a conviction that he should stay in New Salem.

Friends got him a job as postmaster for the village, and he began work in May of 1833. This position gave him a place to stay, in Hill's store, and a small income. Stamps were not yet used: the person who received a letter paid the fee. A single sheet cost six cents for thirty miles, twenty-five cents for four hundred miles. The postmaster kept thirty per cent of the fee and sent the remaining seventy per cent to the mail service.

Now, Abe could read incoming newspapers after the mail arrived each Saturday. He had a growing audience as he read aloud the *Sangamo Journal*, the *Illinois State Register*, and other papers.

He had further good fortune. Mentor Graham chanced to hear that the county surveyor was behind in his work since settlers were arriving daily. So Graham recommended Lincoln as an assistant.

"Abe is not informed in higher mathematics," Graham admitted to Calhoun, the surveyor, "but if you can wait for six weeks, I think I can coach him for you." Calhoun agreed to wait.

Now, again, Lincoln educated himself for a particular task. With Graham's help, Abe studied days and evenings.

In six weeks he bought a compass and surveyor's chain and started work while he continued to study evenings. The surveyor was paid a fee for each piece of land surveyed. Abe's share—plus small fees as postmaster—gave him a fair cash income, so he could pay board and also set aside something toward his debt. "You should forget that store debt," friends told him.

"Surely you don't owe for Berry's share. He's dead."

"He was my partner," Lincoln replied. "I'll pay." And he did pay—though it took many years of saving.

Abe Lincoln made many friends as he tramped the county with Calhoun. His tall, lanky figure and friendly smile were remembered. He was often asked questions about deeds or taxes or sales of lands. He answered those the best he could, and when he did not know, he looked for the answer in the Springfield libraries. One day he bought some legal forms so he could fill out papers for friends. He made no charge for this work of course. He was not licensed to practice law and his advice had no standing. But it was a kindly service, and it helped him educate himself.

Often a friend loaned him a horse and he combined his two jobs. He carried in his straw hat, letters or papers addressed to a farmer living far from the village.

"That's mighty kind of you, Abe!" was his reward.

Motherly wives took an interest in him. "Abe, yer lookin' kinda peaked," one said.

"Abe's fixin' to be a lawyer," her husband remarked. "He's studyin' nights."

When Abe went through Clary's Grove, Mrs. Jack Armstrong had him stay while she "foxed his pants" and fed him a good dinner. She sewed strong buckskin patches on his worn breeches.

Abe liked New Salem life. He had friends all over the county, too.

"You should be a candidate for the Legislature again," Graham told him as summer of 1834 came around. Abe had been thinking of this himself. When local Democrats suggested that they would vote for him, too, he hurried to Springfield to get John Stuart's opinion.

"You're sure of the election, Abe," Stuart said.

This time Lincoln did not write a letter. He went around the county helping with the harvest, talking to friends, and making speeches. In August of 1834, Abraham Lincoln was elected representative for Sangamon County in the State of Illinois.

Only one thing marred Abe Lincoln's pleasure in his prospects. He would be sorry to leave Ann Rutledge. She was engaged to John McNeil, she told him, and John had gone east to fetch his parents and had written a few letters to Ann. Before he left, he had bought a farm eight miles north of New Salem and persuaded James Rutledge to live on it and manage it for him. When Abe went to see Ann after his election she refused to consider breaking her engagement until John should return. But since Rutledge promised to send her away to school, Lincoln consoled himself that perhaps his absence would not matter.

The State Legislature convened on December first. As the day drew near, Lincoln, for the first time in his life, had a serious thought about his appearance. His shabbiness would be no credit to the people he represented. He thought the matter over and then tramped out to see his farmer-friend, Coleman Smoot.

"Did you vote for me, Smoot?" Abe asked directly.

"That I did," Smoot grinned. "And I expect you to do us honor."

"That's what I've come out here about," Lincoln admitted sheepishly. "I wondered"—he glanced down at his shabby, patched breeches, his muddy shoes, and old hat.

"I'll loan you two hundred dollars, Abe," Smoot offered quickly. "Your pay will be three dollars a day; you can return my loan later. Buy yourself a good suit, hat, and shoes and ride to Vandalia in the stagecoach—the state allows you travel expense."

So when Lincoln left for the capital in November, he wore a handsome suit made by a Springfield tailor and he traveled with the other representatives. He would never wear clothes with John Stuart's natural elegance, but neither would he disgrace the people he represented. He meant to do their business well and make himself worthy of their esteem.

CHAPTER TEN

YOUNG LAWMAKER

The driver's horn announced the arrival of the stagecoach in Vandalia, the capital of Illinois. Passengers climbed out wearily, worn by the seventy-five mile journey that had taken two days and a night. Six of these travelers were Sangamon County legislators, among them the tall John Stuart, who was arriving for his second term, and the taller Abraham Lincoln, who came for his first.

Vandalia, a fifteen-year-old town of about eight hundred people, was perched on a bluff above the Kaskaskia River in the southern part of the state.

An example of the kind of top hat that Lincoln would become famous for.

Two important highways crossed there: one connected Washington with the fur-trading center of St. Louis and the other was the north–south road leading from Kentucky to northern Illinois. As Lincoln followed Stuart to the inn, he saw the brick State House, two churches, a few frame buildings around a square, and about a hundred or more log houses along muddy streets. Lamps sparkled in the twilight, and the town was astir to welcome the annual visit of the lawmakers.

Many men greeted Stuart, and he introduced Lincoln as his friend. Lincoln soon saw that this was a help to a newcomer, for Stuart was well liked.

"What's your business?" one member asked Lincoln when they were introduced.

"Oh, I'm a farmer and a riverman," Lincoln grinned at the man, "and a storekeeper, a postmaster, and a surveyor." Men nearby laughed at his droll list, but they thought none the less of him for his many trades. In pioneer times that meant that a man had ambition and was willing to do any useful work in the hope of getting ahead.

During the evening Lincoln's attention was caught by a deep, vibrant voice. He turned and saw nearby a short, handsome, black-haired man who was surrounded by a crowd.

"He's the least man I ever saw," Lincoln remarked to Stuart. "Who is he?"

"That's Stephen A. Douglas, of Morgan County," Stuart whispered. "He is a Vermonter and a Democrat; he came west seeking fame and fortune. I hear he is doing well, too." Stuart introduced the two men, who—with a score of others—talked on state business until late.

The next morning there was a solemn moment when Lincoln was sworn in. The swiftly changing times gave legislators a deep responsibility to the people they represented, and Lincoln resolved to do his best. Good, new laws were sadly needed. The people should have a reliable currency to use in their daily business, and the state needed money in its treasury to pay for roads and schools. These were difficult problems for the lawmakers to solve.

The state of Illinois was sixteen years old, and its northern third was still a wilderness frontier. The village of Chicago was a hamlet of log cabins; some lake traffic had begun and many men claimed that if there was a canal to connect the lake and the Illinois River, settlers would be attracted north and wealth would be created in that wilderness. The population of Illinois had grown from forty-five thousand to two hundred thousand in sixteen years and more people were arriving daily. Usually they settled along the winding rivers because there was no transportation across the prairies. Voters wanted new transportation at once.

Lincoln was a credit to his people in that first term. He served on three committees; he made at least one important speech; and he sponsored and saw passed a bill for building a needed bridge over Salt Creek in his county.

A heavy snow was falling when he returned to New Salem, but his friends came out to welcome him and to praise his success. He recounted tales of behind the scenes in

Vandalia and made them share his pride in lawmaking. They saw that his humor was keen as before, but that otherwise he had changed from the shabby man who had borrowed money for clothes from Smoot. He was as friendly as ever, but he had more confidence in himself.

The next morning Lincoln put on his old clothes and went to work. His jobs as postmaster and surveyor were makeshifts, but they were necessary to earn his living while he studied law. Stuart had planned a course of reading for him, and Lincoln determined to qualify himself as quickly as possible to practice law.

Soon Lincoln went to see Ann Rutledge. She welcomed him and wanted to hear about all he was doing. She had had no letters from her fiancé, but she considered that she was still engaged. Abe Lincoln was in no position to marry; so he was content to see her when he could and to have her friendship.

Then came a tragedy. A deadly illness called "brain fever" spread over Illinois that summer of 1835. Ann was ill—and the doctor said she was dying. When she whispered a wish to see Abe Lincoln, her brother David galloped to fetch him. No one heard the words spoken behind her closed door after Abe came, but Ann's family saw him stumble from the room too dazed to talk.

Soon after that hour, Ann died. Abe thought he could not endure the loss of her friendship—perhaps her love. He could not eat or sleep or work. A friend took him to his farm in the country, where the kindly family cared for him until he began to recover. Fortunately an extra session of the

Legislature was called for that fall, and Lincoln could leave New Salem. Only then did he begin to get back his courage and ambition.

That special session went well and in the summer of 1836, Lincoln announced himself for re-election in a letter printed in the *Sangamo Journal*.

New Salem, June 13, 1836

To the Editor of the Journal:

In your paper of last Saturday, I see a communication over the signature of "Many Voters," in which the candidates who are announced in the Journal, are called upon to "show their hands." Agreed. Here's mine!

I go for all sharing the privileges of government, who assist in bearing its burthens. Consequently I go for admitting all whites to the right of suffrage, who pay taxes or bear arms (by no means excluding females.)

If elected, I shall consider the whole people of Sangamon my constituents, as well those that oppose as those that support me.

While acting as their representative, I shall be governed by their will, on all subjects upon which I have the means of knowing what their will is; and upon all others, I shall do what my own judgment teaches me will best advance their interests. Whether elected or not, I go for distributing the proceeds of the sales of public lands to the several states, to enable our state, in common with others, to dig canals and construct rail roads,

without borrowing money and paying interest on it.
If alive on the first Monday in November, I shall
vote for Hugh L. White for President.

Very respectfully,
A. Lincoln.

That letter was certainly clear enough for all voters to understand. Lincoln knew that Illinois needed transportation, and he announced a practical plan for paying the cost of canals and railroads by the sale of unoccupied public lands. Hugh L. White was the Whig candidate, who was running against the Democrat, Martin Van Buren. The mention of woman's rights, an unpopular subject then, was as daring as Lincoln's stand later for temperance and against slavery.

With this as his platform (though it was not called by that name then) Lincoln campaigned in his district and talked to voters wherever he could get an audience. They liked his straightforwardness, and they approved his record by re-electing him.

One day that same summer, 1836, as Lincoln was striding along the village street he chanced to meet a neighbor, a Mrs. Abell, who was hurrying to the stage.

"I'm going to Kentucky, Abe," she told him. "I'll bring my sister Mary back with me if you'll promise to be my brother-in-law!"

Lincoln recalled Mary Owens; she had visited in New Salem three years before, and he had thought her a pretty girl. Mrs. Abell's jest amused him.

"I accept your proposal," he joked back and helped his neighbor onto the coach.

To his astonishment Mary Owens arrived very soon and she looked fat—not pretty, as he had remembered her. What had he got himself into now, Abe wondered? Did Mary know of her sister's jest? If she did, Mary certainly was willing! Or perhaps she just happened to come? Was he supposed to propose? Did he want her? Those were enough questions to daunt any lawyer. He was glad when it was time to leave for Vandalia.

That winter there were more legislators from Sangamon County, because the population in the district had increased; nine men took the stage for the capital. As they climbed aboard someone noticed that they were all tall men and hastily counted up their total height as fifty-four feet, an average of six feet per man.

"They're our 'Long Nine!'" the crowd yelled, and the nickname clung. That group, "The Long Nine," was one of the famous groups in Illinois political history. Their instructions this day when they left were clear and plain; they were to vote for "internal improvements" and to have the state capital moved to Springfield.

This question of which city should be the state capital had been talked about for some time. The State House at Vandalia was small and shabby; a new one must be built somewhere. Many people thought that Vandalia was too far south in a state that was rapidly developing northward. Several Illinois towns were working for the honor (and the lively business) that being the capital brought to a town, but Springfield, in the center of the state, thought she had the best claim.

John Stuart had not run for re-election in 1836 because he hoped to be elected to the Congress of the United States; so Abraham Lincoln became the Whig leader in the House. He kept a watchful eye on every bill for a railroad, a bridge, or a canal. There would not be money for all that were needed— why not see to it that counties favoring Springfield for the capital should have their good sense rewarded? With masterly political skill Lincoln arranged daytime conferences and midnight sessions. When others of the Long Nine despaired, he thought up some new strategy and showed amazing resourcefulness and patience.

As the session neared its end, feeling grew intense; sometimes it seemed certain that Alton or Jacksonville would be chosen. But it all turned out as Lincoln had planned. The improvements were allotted over the state (as was wise) and on the twenty-eighth of February, 1837, Springfield was voted the capital of Illinois.

On the very next day an important letter was delivered to Lincoln, a letter that told him his application was accepted, and that now he was licensed to practice law in Illinois. The backwoods boy with "no education" was now an attorney at law.

When the stagecoach arrived in Springfield a few days later, the Long Nine were met by a delighted crowd who hailed Abe Lincoln as a hero. There were dinners and many speeches, and leading businessmen urged Lincoln to move to Springfield.

"A man of your ability should not bury himself in a village," Joshua Speed, the merchant, said. "We need you here." Speed's smile and friendliness spoke even more than his words. But Lincoln made no promise. He went up to New Salem.

There old neighbors welcomed him. But he saw that he could never make a good living at law in a village. And Mary Owens was still there. He had corresponded with her during the winter, but when he saw her, he didn't want her—and she seemed so willing!

In 1831 Abe Lincoln had known in his heart that he should stay in New Salem. Now with equal sureness he knew that the time had come to leave. He packed saddlebags, borrowed a horse, rode to Springfield, and went straight to Joshua Speed's store.

"How much will a bedstead cost me?" was his greeting to the merchant.

"About seventeen dollars," Speed said, smiling. Lincoln's shoulders drooped.

"Cheap as you think that is," he admitted, "I do not have the money. If you would make me a loan, I'll repay you as soon as my law business is a success."

"I know a better plan," Speed said. "I have a large room and a double bed. You are welcome to share both."

"Where is your room?" Lincoln said, his face brightening.

"Upstairs!" Speed grinned as he jerked his thumb toward the stairway.

Lincoln picked up his saddlebags, dashed up the stairs, and set them on the floor in Speed's room. In half a minute, he was back, his face beaming.

"Well, Speed," he reported, "I'm moved!"

Customers entered the store just then, and Lincoln went out to look the town over. Spring mud was still deep, and there were no sidewalks. As he leaped over one of the worst puddles, he bumped into his friend William Butler, the clerk of the Sangamon Circuit Court.

"Abe Lincoln!" Butler exclaimed, grabbing at Lincoln's arm. "Are you in Springfield to stay?"

Lincoln nodded. "I came today," he said.

"You're having dinner with me," Butler invited. Lincoln went home with him. He took his meals at Butler's home the four years that he roomed with Joshua Speed.

And so Abraham Lincoln came to Springfield, the new capital of Illinois. He was twenty-eight years old, a licensed lawyer, respected by the people who knew him, loved by his many friends. The "backwoods boy" had left the forests just after his twenty-first birthday. Now, seven years later, the "handy man" of many trades had left the pioneer village and settled in one of the thriving towns of the great Middle West.

A letter from Joshua F. Speed to Abraham Lincoln, dated Tuesday, May 6, 1862.

CHAPTER ELEVEN

MR. LINCOLN OF SPRINGFIELD

Springfield had changed a great deal in the six years since Abe Lincoln first saw it when he looked for Denton Offutt. From a cluster of log cabins it had grown to be a town of fifteen hundred people, and it served a farm community of perhaps eighteen thousand. In this year, 1837, the town had six churches, good schools and an academy for advanced students, two newspapers, many stores, and several small factories. Prosperous families lived in good frame houses, and there was an air of vitality about the place.

Abraham Lincoln's birthplace, Hodgenville, Kentucky.

Lincoln went directly to his friend John Stuart, who had promised a partnership in law when Abe came to Springfield. These two young men—one so aristocratic, the other of humble birth—were congenial; and soon a new sign hung from Stuart's second-story office window. The *Sangamo Journal* printed their announcement:

> *J. T. Stuart and A. Lincoln, Attorneys and Counsellors at Law, will practice, conjointly, in the Courts of this Judicial Circuit Office, No. 4 Hoffman's Row, upstairs, Springfield, April 12, 1837.*

Their office was a small, dingy room, scantily furnished but conveniently located directly above the Circuit Court room. Here Abraham Lincoln began practicing his new profession. The days when everyone called him "Abe" were gone. He was now "Mr. Lincoln," a promising young attorney of Springfield. Perhaps he felt this subtle change, for a few mornings later he ran his fingers through his unruly hair and decided to have it trimmed. He had noticed a sign, "Billy the Barber," near the corner. He clattered down the stairs and entered the little shop.

"Good morning, Mr. Lincoln," the barber greeted him. "What can I do for you?"

"You know me?" Lincoln exclaimed in surprise. "I came for a haircut."

"Yes, I know you; sit here, sir," the barber said. "I shall never forget your kindness to me when I was in need."

Lincoln eyed the dark-skinned face, and memory stirred. While Billy cut the untidy hair, Lincoln listened.

"It was in the fall of 1831, I remember," the man said, "and late evening. I had been hunting near St. Louis and had come back up the Illinois River and the Sangamon. In sight of a small village, I fell in with a tall man who wore a red shirt and carried an ax—you, sir. The village was New Salem."

"I do remember," Lincoln seemed pleased. "You are a native of Haiti. You had lived in Baltimore and then in New Orleans"—the incident was coming back now. "But you found living difficult for a free Negro, so you moved to St. Louis."

William de Fleurville snipped diligently, proud that this important man recalled him.

"You have it right, Mr. Lincoln. You took me to the inn where you were boarding. You put me up, and you mentioned my trade to your friends. Before the evening ended I had clipped a dozen heads, and when I left the next morning I had a comfortable jingle of change in my pockets. Your kindness helped me to decide on settling here, and Illinois has proved to be a good place for me. I like the people. I've had this shop for five years. I hear you are an attorney now; I wonder if you would write up a deed for me, Mr. Lincoln?"

"A deed?" Again Lincoln was surprised; he had not heard of a black man buying property.

"Yes, sir. I have saved some money, and I plan to buy town lots. I would count it as a favor if you will do my legal business."

"I'll be glad to," Lincoln assured him.

Other men dropped in. Lincoln saw that the place was popular. The prices were reasonable; Lincoln decided to come often.

Back in the new office he went at the legal work. Stuart turned over everything he could to his new partner because he meant to put more of his own time into politics. He planned to run for the United States Congress the next year, and he was determined to defeat the Democrat—Stephen A. Douglas. A new lawyer could not ask for a better opportunity than Lincoln had in that office.

The law part of the business was easy for Lincoln, but he hated the bookkeeping. Because Stuart was often away, there must be some keeping of records. Lincoln was ever quick with an idea to save work. Now, when a client paid a fee, Lincoln put one half of the money into an envelope on which he marked the client's name and the total fee. The other half of the money he put into his own pocket.

When Stuart returned Lincoln reported on the court work and then added, "And here's your money, John."

"Money?" Stuart stared at the envelopes Lincoln handed him. Lincoln explained, and they had a good laugh as Stuart pocketed his share.

During that first spring and summer in Springfield, Lincoln corresponded with Mary Owens, but their "romance" made no progress. She didn't say "yes" or "no" for the very good reason that he did not ask the important question. At last he decided to propose—and Mary promptly said "no." Her promptness was disconcerting after all his worry, but at least the vexing business was now settled. And there was much to interest him in Springfield.

The Young Men's Lyceum was a popular debating society, and Lincoln was invited to join. He wrote letters and articles for the Springfield newspapers and sometimes amused himself by signing a fanciful name. His style of writing was clear, and he wrote straightforwardly or in a tone of satire, as he chose. If he had not happened to be more interested in law and politics, he might easily have won fame as a writer.

But the stirring times made politics fascinating. He decided to run again for the State Legislature. When he went out to campaign, he discovered that his previous record and his newspaper writing had made his name known and he had a big audience.

This year both parties held campaign meetings. One of the Democratic speakers was the elegant Colonel Taylor who talked about "horny hands of toil" and made slurring remarks about "aristocratic Whigs."

"I'll take the wind out of that fellow's sails," Lincoln said in annoyance. He edged near to the colonel and deftly jerked his waistcoat.

The garment burst open, displaying a fancy ruffled shirt and a glittering watch chain that dripped with jewels and golden seals. The audience roared as Taylor nervously hunted buttons. Lincoln's turn for speaking came a few minutes later.

"While Colonel Taylor was making these charges against the Whigs over the country, riding in fine carriages, wearing ruffled shirts, kid gloves, and massive watch chains with large gold seals, and flourishing a heavy gold-headed cane, I was a poor boy, hired on a flatboat at eight dollars a month, and had only one pair of breeches to my back, and they were buckskin. Now, if you know the nature of buckskin when wet and dried by the sun, it will shrink; and my breeches kept shrinking until they left several inches of my legs bare between the tops of my socks and the lower part of my breeches. And whilst I was growing taller, they were becoming shorter and so much tighter that they left a blue streak around my legs that can be seen to this day. If you call that aristocracy, I plead guilty to the charge." The crowd enjoyed that!

Another campaign meeting was held in the courtroom just below the Stuart & Lincoln law office. The speaker said some bitter things, and the editor of a Springfield newspaper was angered.

"Pull him down!" the editor yelled and pushed his way forward.

At that instant the amazed audience saw a pair of long legs appear from the ceiling. A second later Lincoln's tall figure landed *plunk* from the trap door onto the platform. He motioned for silence, but the uproar increased. He edged to the speaker's table, grabbed a heavy water pitcher, and waved it threateningly.

"Hold on, gentlemen!" he shouted, and his high, penetrating voice quieted them. "This is a land of free speech, and Mr. Baker has a right to be heard. I am here to protect him, and no man shall take him from this stand if I can prevent it."

The audience was shocked to silence, and Baker finished his talk. The right of free speech had been granted by the Constitution, as Mr. Lincoln reminded that audience, but people had had little training in listening to the "other side." When a speaker spoke unpopular words, he was hissed and booed—and often stoned. Abraham Lincoln was one of the first public men who taught people to listen to both sides of a question.

That summer of 1838 Lincoln was re-elected to the State Legislature, and his leadership of his party strengthened. He barely missed being chosen speaker of the house, although the state was strongly Democratic.

He was elected again in 1840 and took his seat in the handsome new State House in Springfield. Fellow townsmen spoke of him with pride and predicted a bright future.

CHAPTER TWELVE

CONGRESSMAN LINCOLN

John Stuart was elected to Congress at that same time and Lincoln was proud, though he regretted that it would take his partner away from Springfield much of each year. Lincoln modestly doubted that he could manage alone; so the two friends decided to end the partnership in April of 1841.

Soon after that, Lincoln formed a new partnership with Stephen T. Logan. Lincoln knew Logan well; knew that he was exacting, strict about manners, a dour Scot, and orderly to a fault.

Abraham Lincoln while campaigning for the U.S. Senate, taken in Chicago, Illinois.

But Logan knew law. For three years Lincoln kept records, copied briefs perfectly, made the room orderly, and sat upright with his feet on the floor. He did not pretend to like this training; but he liked to learn what the training taught him.

Outside of the office Lincoln enjoyed himself. The capital city was very gay. Since travel was tedious and expensive, legislators stayed in Springfield through the whole session; they brought with them their wives and pretty daughters. Belles in Virginia and Kentucky wangled invitations and arrived with their loveliest frocks, sure of many beaux.

Among the visitors was Mary Todd, daughter of a Kentucky gentleman and sister of a popular Springfield hostess, Mrs. Ninian W. Edwards. Abraham Lincoln was attracted to the visitor. Mary Todd was small and vivacious, with snapping dark eyes and a gay manner. In her charming dress of white net tied with a black velvet sash and neckband, she was the center of an admiring group at her sister's party. Mary Todd had a ready wit and a keen mind—as well as bright eyes and a pretty smile. A dozen young men sought her company and persuaded her to stay for a long visit.

Lincoln courted her diligently, and Mary Todd seemed to like him—indeed, why not? He was mentioned as a distinguished politician, a successful lawyer, and a man sure to succeed. She saw for herself that he was friendly, witty, and admired. In the summer of 1840 they were engaged. But soon after Christmas their engagement was broken. Mary Todd held her head high and did not explain. Lincoln was so depressed he could hardly work. Joshua Speed, who was selling his store to go back to Kentucky, decided something should be done for his friend.

"You must go to my old home, Abe," he announced firmly. "Mother will make you well."

So Lincoln went to Farmington, the beautiful Speed home stead near Louisville. Mrs. Speed fed him and mothered him. Joshua's sister, Mary Speed, walked and read and joked with him until his spirits and health improved and he could go back to his work.

It chanced that part of his return journey was aboard the riverboat S.S. *Lebanon*, between Louisville and St. Louis. From the upper deck Lincoln looked down upon a group of slaves, chained together. The sight saddened Lincoln. He wrote to Mary Speed about his feeling against slaveholding, and he never forgot the hateful scene.

Slavery had not been a problem in Illinois; the state was a part of the Northwest Territory, and by the Ordinance of 1787 slavery was not allowed. The northern part of the state was largely settled by easterners who came by way of the Great Lakes. They wanted slavery abolished. In the southern part most of the people were from slave-holding states and were used to slavery; some even favored it though they had moved north. Illinois statesmen kept slavery out of politics; that was not hard to do, for new settlers were busy with their own affairs. Lincoln had made his opinion clear early in his political career; he believed that slavery was an evil, but he did not favor abolition as the remedy. Now, haunted by the sad scene on the boat, he pondered often about how to end the injustice of enslaving fellow men.

Back in Springfield Lincoln pitched into his law business determined to think no more about Mary Todd. But he was restless and unhappy. After a time a friend brought the lovers together, and they made up their differences and renewed their engagement.

In November of 1842 they were married. The wedding was small, and they took no honeymoon journey; for Lincoln was still a poor man, burdened with old debts. He and Mary went directly to the Globe Tavern near the Square in Springfield, where they lived for some time. The stagecoach station was on the ground floor of this tavern, and on the arrival of a coach a bell was rung loudly, calling the coach boys to bring out new horses. But Mary did not mind the confusion: she liked being in the center of things. And she was fascinated with her husband's work. She read books and reviewed them for him; she entertained visitors and promoted his career in every way she knew. Lincoln had decided not to run for the State Legislature again. He felt that his long service deserved a step up; and since Stuart chose not to run again, Lincoln expected to be nominated for Congress.

To his mortification, he was elected, instead, as a delegate to the district convention and instructed to vote for his good friend, Edward Baker. That was a trick of fate he had not expected!

"I feel a good deal like a fellow who is made a groomsman to a man that has cut him out and is marrying his own dear gal!" he told a friend.

In 1844, though he was not running for office himself, he toured Illinois and southern Indiana, speaking for the

Whigs. He saw many old friends and addressed a large audience at Rockport. Two years later Lincoln was elected to Congress after a hard campaign against the popular preacher, Peter Cartwright. But the fight, the long postponement of the honor, and the threat of war with Mexico took away the joy of victory.

Meanwhile, Lincoln's personal life had been happy, and he was being successful in his profession. In 1844 he left the Logan office and invited young William Herndon (a cousin of the Rowan Herndon of New Salem) to be his partner in a new firm "Lincoln & Herndon." Billy Herndon was young, well educated, intelligent, and devoted to Lincoln. Even more important, he was willing to do many of the office chores that Lincoln hated. They prospered. Lincoln's old debts were paid off; and he began to get ahead.

The Lincolns' first son, Robert Todd, was born while they lived at the Globe Tavern; but soon after, Lincoln bought an attractive story-and-a-half house at the corner of Jackson and Eighth streets. Their second son, named for Lincoln's friend, Edward Baker, was born in the new home.

It was from the house on Jackson Street that the Lincolns left for Washington in the late autumn of 1847.

They found the capital city a strange conglomeration of squalor and beauty. The White House was a dignified mansion and the unfinished Capitol building promised to be beautiful some day. One side of Pennsylvania Avenue had a sidewalk and was the fashionable promenade, but elsewhere people picked their way through dust or mud. Hogs, geese, and chickens ran around freely, seeking tossed-out garbage.

MARY TODD LINCOLN

Mary Todd Lincoln was a very complex woman, with many unusual personality traits.

She was born and raised in Lexington, Kentucky, to a relatively wealthy family. Her family owned slaves and several of her half brothers were killed while serving in the Confederate Army.

She went to finishing school and was fluent in French. Before marrying Abraham Lincoln, Mary Todd was courted by Stephen A. Douglas, who would later become Abraham Lincoln's chief political rival, defeating Lincoln in the U.S. Senate race, and losing to Lincoln in the presidential election of 1860. Mary's family greatly preferred Douglas, but Mary was attracted to Lincoln because they shared a love of literature and Whig politics.

Mary suffered from migraine headaches and may have had emotional problems with depression or bipolar disorder— or both. Throughout her life she was very moody and was often in conflict with her husband and sons.

After her husband's assassination, Mary was forced to write letters to Congress in order to receive a small pension on which to live.

In 1871, she jumped from a window to escape an imagined fire and was committed to a private institution by her son Robert Todd. She eventually was released to her sister, Elizabeth Edwards, and lived with her until Mary's death in 1882.

They brushed their grimy bodies against silken skirts unless parasols were used quickly to poke the creatures away.

The spires of several churches caught one's eye, but there were also many saloons and gambling houses. Gangs of shackled slaves shuffled through the streets, and an open slave market near the Capitol was offensive. Lincoln was disappointed, where he had expected to be proud. Fortunately the chatter of small boys was diverting as they drove to the boardinghouse where they were to live.

Mrs. Lincoln had high hopes of social success in Washington. But she found that President Polk was neither stylish nor elegant, and there was little formal entertaining. Worse still, her husband was soon involved in unpleasant arguments about the Mexican War.

The causes of this war went back to the Louisiana Purchase when the United States bought that vast area of unsurveyed land. No one knew exactly whether the boundary was the Rio Grande or the Nueces River. Lincoln made a plain statement of the facts in his speech before Congress in January of 1848:

"... As to the country now in question (Texas) we bought it of France in 1803, and sold it to Spain in 1819.... After this, all Mexico, including Texas, revolutionized against Spain; still later, Texas revolutionized against Mexico." Abraham Lincoln knew his country's history.

Through all these changes the boundaries of Texas didn't matter because no one lived there. When people from the North set up homes and businesses and asked that Texas be admitted as a state, the boundary was important. Both Mexican and United States armies moved to the land between the rivers and the President declared war.

The shooting began after Mr. Lincoln was nominated for Congress and was over when he went to take his seat in December of 1847. But American soldiers were still there, peace papers were not signed, and Congress must vote money to finish the task. This Lincoln did.

But when he was asked to support resolutions which said the President was right to declare war, he balked. Congress, not the President, had the right to declare war, he said. If one man, though President, had the right to make war, where was the difference between that and the hated right of kings?

He was concerned, too, about his country getting more southern land—and probably more slavery.

"Show me the spot where there was Mexican aggression!" Lincoln said.

Political opponents twisted his words to mean that he would not support American soldiers. They called him "Spotty Lincoln" in derision. Many Illinois newspapers did not even print copies of his speech and his letters explaining his convictions. What hurt most was that Billy Herndon, his partner and close friend, was *against* him! That was hard to endure.

In a long letter to Herndon, Lincoln explained what he thought about that war and then wrote, "I will stake my life that if you had been in my place you would have voted just as I did. Would you have voted for what you felt and knew to be a lie? I know you would not." On the "direct question of the Justice of the war . . . no man can be silent if he would. You are compelled to speak; your only alternative is to tell the truth or a lie." Where truth was concerned, "Honest Abe" saw no problem.

Lincoln's firm stand for what he believed right injured his prospects in Washington and in Illinois. His wife suffered deeply. In the summer she and the boys paid a long visit to her family in Kentucky. While she was away, Mr. and Mrs. Lincoln wrote to each other letters about themselves and their beloved sons and things that are important to a man and woman who love each other. They must have valued those letters for several of them were saved.

The term in Congress was not all loss. Mr. Lincoln made some good speeches; he widened his circle of friends; and he gained valuable experience. He attended the Whig convention where Zachary Taylor, the general of Mexican War fame, was nominated for president, and he campaigned for Taylor in New England. Lincoln did not run for re-election to Congress. No fanfare greeted Lincoln when he came back to Springfield. Illinois Whigs thought he had hurt his party and ended his political career. After his dreams and his wife's determination that he should get to high places, this was hard to take.

As he leaned back in the worn chair in his office, did he think of the Abe Lincoln who had drifted down the Sangamon that July day in 1831? That boy would have called this man a success. He was a prosperous lawyer; he had a devoted wife and two sons. But somewhere in the nineteen years the dream had changed. Ambitious Abraham Lincoln now aimed higher than being a good lawyer. But he saw no way of achieving the new goal.

"The best thing for me to do now," he told himself, "is to drop politics for good and get at my law business."

CHAPTER THIRTEEN

RIDING THE CIRCUIT

Their house on Jackson Street looked wonderful to the Lincolns after that crowded boardinghouse in Washington. Bob and Eddie looked up their friends. Neighbors came to call on Mrs. Lincoln and to hear about the latest news and fashions. Mr. Lincoln had gone to his office.

That Lincoln and Herndon office was a dingy place, for Billy Herndon was no more orderly than Lincoln; but their partnership was congenial and they could overcome differences of opinion. Lincoln was now forty years old—and he called his partner "Billy"; Herndon was thirty-one—

The Lincoln summer home in Washington, D.C.

and he always spoke of the senior partner as "Mr. Lincoln." Their prospects for business were fine. A client felt a certain distinction when his case was handled by a man who had served in Congress. Shades of political opinion didn't matter in court. Lincoln's wide acquaintance brought clients from a distance, and he had work in the Eighth Circuit courts as well as in Sangamon County.

Circuit courts had been set up in the state to serve citizens who lived in thinly settled communities where court was needed only occasionally. Most pioneer disputes were about boundaries, wills, or debts, and could wait until a judge came for a few days each spring and fall. This judge went from one community to the next in a kind of circle tour called a "circuit" so he came to be called the "Judge of the Circuit Court." There were no railroads, so the judge must ride a horse or drive a light buggy. He was said to be "riding the circuit" when he made his trips. Usually one or two lawyers went along with him. If the case was important, they were hired ahead of time so they could look up the law in their books in Springfield.

Judge David Davis was on the circuit around Springfield. He was a tall man, and he weighed more than three hundred pounds. He rode in a light buggy and sometimes Lincoln crowded his lean frame in beside the judge, though it was more comfortable to ride horseback alongside. Nights, the men stayed with friends or stopped at miserable little inns. Rain, cold, poor food, and long hours on a road that often was a mere trail across the prairie made the work hard. But Lincoln did not mind hardship, and he liked to be with people.

Herndon stayed in Springfield and did the work there during circuit court time.

Farm living had changed in the twenty years since Thomas Lincoln's family had moved to Illinois. Now some farmers lived in frame houses and kept horses instead of oxen. Many used steel plows and some had reaping machines made in Chicago at the new McCormick factory.

Court week was as good as a fair. People managed their work so they could come to town and see the judge arrive. If a man knew anyone who had a case up for trial, he might bring his whole family and visit a relative for the week—if he was lucky enough to have a relative and someone to stay at home and tend the stock. When Judge Davis's buggy pulled up at the courthouse, men rushed over to engage a lawyer or talk to the judge.

A famous case during the years Lincoln was riding the circuit was the trial of "Duff" Armstrong for the murder of a man named Metzker. Duff was a son of Jack Armstrong, the Clary Grove leader Lincoln had fought in New Salem. His wife, Hannah, was the woman who had "foxed" Abe's breeches when he tore them on brambles while surveying. Metzker was killed (or had died) during a camp meeting the summer before. The story was that James Norris had hit him on the head with a club and that Duff Armstrong finished him off with a slingshot. Norris had already been tried and pronounced guilty—mostly on the testimony of a Charles Allen who claimed he saw the whole thing.

Lincoln thought it a slim story and believed in Duff's innocence, but it would be a hard case to prove and was made worse by the verdict against Norris. The Armstrongs were nearly wild with worry; their only comfort was that Abe Lincoln had agreed to take the case. But when he arrived Lincoln offered them no bright hopes. He merely spoke a few friendly words to Hannah.

As the trial began, observers noticed that Lincoln was trying for a jury of young men.

"Bet he thinks young fellows will understand the fix Duff is in," one man whispered.

Then the state put Charles Allen on the stand, and he told the long tale that had convicted Norris. Anxiously Hannah watched Lincoln. He sat quietly, his eyes on the ceiling. She wondered whether he was even listening.

In the afternoon, when he began to cross-examine the witness, he asked such trivial questions that Hannah despaired; the knuckles of her clinched hands were white. Why didn't Abe do something before it was too late? But wait! She straightened up. His questions were coming faster, now.

"Did you actually see the fight?"

"Yes, sir." Allen's answer was firm.

"Where were you at the time?"

"Not far away—about one hundred and fifty feet, I'd guess."

"Describe the weapon."

Allen went into detail, describing the slingshot Duff was supposed to have used.

"What time was this?" Lincoln asked casually.

"Before midnight. Around eleven o'clock."

Lincoln paused and squinted one eye inquiringly. "How could you see that far, in the night?"

"The moon was bright—a full moon. High in the sky, as bright as day."

Lincoln whirled suddenly to face the sheriff.

"Hand me that book—there, that one," Lincoln pointed to a small paper book he had put on the table with other papers. He opened the book slowly. Men nearby saw by the cover that it was an almanac. Lincoln held it so those close to him could see the page as he read. On the night of the supposed murder the moon was in the first quarter and had set before midnight. The crowd was silent in shocked astonishment. The idea was so plain—yet no one had thought of it. Hannah flushed, hopeful for the first time.

The fight was not over, but with Allen proved a liar, Duff now had a chance. Lincoln next proved that the slingshot showed in court was not Duff's and was in another man's pocket the night of the murder.

At last the time came for Lincoln's summing up for the jury. The crowded courtroom was stifling when he rose to speak. Seated, Lincoln did not look taller than other men. But as he unfolded his long legs he seemed to tower over everyone in that room. He took off his coat and vest and hung them on a chair. The room was so quiet that a dog's bark outside sounded loud. He unwound the stock from about his neck and began to speak. At once his gray eyes brightened; his expression became alert; his high tenor voice carried to every corner and to the listening crowds at windows and doors. Men who heard boasted afterward that it was the best speech Lincoln ever made.

He talked an hour, reviewing evidence, pointing out that Metzker might have died from a fall he'd had off his horse. He told of his long friendship for the Armstrong family and his belief in their fine characters.

"I am interested only in justice," he ended. "I am trying this case for friendship—not a fee." (Many lawyers charged a big fee for a murder case. Working without any pay was unusual and impressive.)

The jury acquitted Duff on the first ballot. Hannah sobbed with joy and could hardly speak when Lincoln came to bid her good-bye.

Fees for legal work in the Circuit Court were low, since most cases were fairly unimportant. But they counted up. Lincoln was making a good living through these years and saving money. He got a few large fees, too; a thousand dollars for a patent case connected with the McCormick reaper, five thousand for a tax case for the Illinois Central Railroad. Between sessions of the Circuit Court he practiced law in Springfield.

About a year after the Lincolns came back from Washington, the family was saddened by the death of little Eddie. That same year, 1850, a third son, William Wallace, was born. Three years later, in 1853, they had a fourth son, named Thomas for Lincoln's father, who had died. Young Thomas was affectionately called "Tad"; he was a lively little boy who spoke with a lisp. The small home seemed full of boys; and since Lincoln was doing well, the house was enlarged to a full two stories. They were very comfortable.

Mrs. Lincoln was busy with her family, as mothers are. She made clothes for the boys and for herself, and she cooked the meals. Sometimes she had a "girl" to help with cleaning and picking up; there was plenty of that. The church sewing society often had meetings at the Lincoln home, and Mrs. Lincoln entertained guests she thought would help her husband. He had no political ambitions now, but she wanted to help him in his profession. When she had company she liked to have things "nice." But that was not easy, because Mr. Lincoln allowed the boys to be as rowdy as they pleased. Often Mrs. Lincoln had bad headaches, and then she was cross and miserable. Her husband would take the boys for a long walk to keep the house quiet until she got better.

Mr. Lincoln helped at home as other men did. He went to market with a big basket, which he lugged home and set on the kitchen table. He chopped wood and kept fires going. That fancy new stove in the parlor, called a "Parlour Temple," fairly gobbled up wood, but Mrs. Lincoln thought it very stylish. Mr. Lincoln took care of the horse that he had bought for riding the circuit, and he milked the cow.

That cow sometimes made trouble. Lincoln kept it tied to a sycamore tree in the meadow a block or so from the house. Boys in the neighborhood, including his own, played ball nearby; and often when Mr. Lincoln went to milk he forgot what he came to do and played with them. On an evening when the Lincolns were having a party, the cook needed milk. Lincoln had done the milking, but when the game got exciting he joined in.

Small Willie came running from the house. "The milk," he yelled. "They want the milk!"

Lincoln tossed the bat aside, grabbed the bucket of milk and dashed for the house as fast as his long legs could get him there. The boys marveled that he could run fast without spilling. That was a skill he had learned lugging water in Indiana.

Through the early fifties Abraham Lincoln was successful and content. He was still ambitious, and so was his wife. But law was a challenge to an ambitious man and promised a great future. The threat to the Union of slavery spreading, not personal ambition, drew him back into politics.

This threat became important when Kansas and Nebraska were to be organized as territories. Opinion was divided as to whether the large part of the Louisiana Purchase should be "slave" or free." Under the Missouri Compromise they would be "free." Senator Stephen A. Douglas introduced a bill which abolished the Missouri Compromise and provided that each state should decide about slavery for itself. The bill passed and became a law.

This Missouri Compromise had long been one of America's important documents. It had been adopted in 1820 when the territory of Missouri had asked to be a state. Up to that year the new republic had not been troubled about slavery. The

Mrs. Norah Gridley, cousin of Mrs. Abraham Lincoln, and Miss May Coleman, at the typewriter, outside of and near the corner of the Lincoln Cabin, a log cabin in Illinois that was built by Thomas Lincoln and visited by his son, Abraham Lincoln.

cotton-growing South had slaves. The more industrial East had about ended their slaveholding, and the whole Northwest Territory—Ohio, Indiana, Illinois, Michigan, and Wisconsin were "free." But the huge Louisiana Purchase had made a new problem. What should that region be? Northerners knew that if it had slavery, then a majority of the states would be slaveholding. Southerners knew that if all that land was "free" the institution of slavery would gradually die out.

The quarrel over admitting Missouri in 1820 had almost broken up the Union. Abe Lincoln was too young then to understand, but he learned about it later. Finally, both sides gave up something and a compromise was made. The people who were against slavery had agreed that Missouri could be admitted as a slaveholding state. The people who favored slavery had given up hope of controlling more states in the north. Together they had agreed about future states to be formed from Louisiana-Purchase land; a state that was north of an east-west line drawn about where the Ohio River entered the Mississippi should be "free" and states that were south of that line could be "slave." This compromise had held for more than thirty years, until Douglas's Nebraska bill, based on what he called "popular sovereignty," set it aside. Many, like Lincoln, believed that this bill would quickly allow slavery to spread.

Stephen A. Douglas had been elected in 1852 for his second term in the United States Senate, so he was not a candidate in 1854. But he took an active part in the campaign for state legislators in Illinois. Douglas was an excellent speaker and probably the most promising politician of that year. He was devoted to his country; and many people likened him to Henry Clay. He was mentioned as a good man for the next president, though some thought that in writing his Nebraska bill he was over-influenced by personal interests and ambition.

Abraham Lincoln, though busy and successful in his law practice, proposed to bring an understanding of that Nebraska Bill to the people. He began by writing letters to influential friends and by making speeches. He pointed out two errors in Douglas's reasoning: first, when part of the people were slaves true "popular sovereignty" was impossible because the slave part of the population could not vote; second, allowing new states to decide for or against slavery was an attempt to evade an evil. Lincoln believed that the time was approaching when the nation must decide about slavery, because no country could long exist half slave and half free.

In October of 1854 Lincoln explained his ideas in a speech in Peoria. He told the whole history of the Missouri Compromise and pointed out the danger of setting it aside. Listeners saw that Lincoln's oratory had improved; he did less clowning, and his manner was dignified. He still illustrated a point with a story, but his tales were brief and well chosen. His eyes lighted when he talked, and his friendly manner was pleasing. That speech was printed and was widely read. Anti-Nebraska voters won a majority in the legislature, and Lincoln just missed being chosen as United States Senator.

In that same year, 1854, many men who had been Whigs joined with some anti-Nebraska Democrats to form a new party. They gave it a name Thomas Jefferson had used— Republican. Most Republicans were against slavery and, like Lincoln, were firmly against allowing slavery to spread. Most Democrats were for the right to hold slaves. In May of 1856, Lincoln allied himself with this new Republican party when he spoke at a state convention in Bloomington. That address was so thrilling that reporters forgot their pencils in eager listening; and as Lincoln had no notes, it became known as the "Lost Speech." Some said that it was the best of all Lincoln's speeches. So remarkable was its effect that twenty-one days later Lincoln, who was hardly known beyond Illinois, received several votes for the nomination for vice-president.

But Lincoln himself, though ambitious, did not push his advantage. It seemed, almost, as though he was waiting— waiting. And while he waited, something in him began to grow, some secret, hidden stir of spirit. He pondered about his country and about the idea of government his country stood for. He wondered what might happen if men let the nation drift along, half free.

To a friend he wrote, "The problem is too much for me. May God in His mercy superintend a solution."

In June of 1858 a Republican State Convention in Springfield endorsed Lincoln for the United States Senate. Afterward he addressed the convention, giving what came to be known as the "House Divided" speech. It was so stirring that he became the favored Republican candidate. Douglas's second term in the Senate was ending, and the legislature elected that year would have to decide between these two men.

Senator Douglas was to speak in Chicago on the 9th of July. Lincoln was in the city and went to hear the speech.

The audience stood in the street in front of the Tremont Hotel to hear Douglas argue in plausible fashion that men should be allowed to manage their own property as they chose. If a man wanted to have slaves, that was his affair, and the government had no business to dictate. He was so eloquent that listeners hardly realized he was saying that human beings whose skin happened to be black were property the same as oxen or wagons.

As Abraham Lincoln listened, an urge to answer those arguments came over him. The secret feeling that had been growing in him told him that now, now was the time he had been waiting for! Lincoln determined to answer Douglas at once.

Early the next morning he demanded of the committee the right to state the other side of the case at that same place, "this very evening!"

Dismayed, they told him the time was too short, but when he insisted, the meeting was arranged.

That evening of July 10th, the street in front of the Tremont Hotel was thronged with people. Rockets whirled to the heavens. A band played stirring tunes. Crowds burst into loud cheers when Abraham Lincoln stepped onto the balcony. "Lincoln!" "Listen to Old Abe!" "He'll tell 'em!" men shouted.

Lincoln made a brilliant speech that held the vast crowd. He repeated parts of his Springfield speech—"A house divided against itself cannot stand . . . this government cannot endure permanently, half slave and half free," and he explained his reasons for his belief. He ended the long address with these words, "I leave you, hoping that the lamp of Liberty will burn in your bosoms until there shall no longer be a doubt that all men are created equal."

The crowd roared its approval.

Would Abraham Lincoln give up politics? After this night his tall plug hat was tossed directly into the political ring.

• CHAPTER FOURTEEN •

DEBATES AND CONVENTIONS

Illinois was a very exciting place to live in that summer of 1858. The campaign promised to be lively even though it was not the year for a presidential election. Democrats endorsed Senator Douglas to succeed himself. The new Republican party approved Abraham Lincoln for the same office. Men who had heard or read the speeches made in Chicago wanted to hear both candidates.

Newspapers took up the idea. Lincoln challenged Douglas to public debate. Douglas finally consented, and a committee planned seven

The Coles County Courthouse in Charleston, Illinois.

meetings and made rules. Douglas was to open the first debate and every other one afterward. Lincoln was to open the second, fourth, and sixth. The opener was to talk an hour—then his opponent an hour and a half—with the opener having a final half hour.

In August, Lincoln went to Ottawa for the first debate, on a special train of seventeen coaches. He had been in this town during the Black Hawk War, but it had grown so in twenty-six years that he would not have known it. A committee met him and escorted him to a carriage that had been decorated with evergreens by a committee of young ladies. The procession of bands, military companies, and political clubs was a half mile long. Douglas arrived at the other end of town and the two men were taken to lunch at fine houses in the same block. The debate lasted all afternoon.

Next morning newspaper headlines reported:

THE GREAT DEBATE AT OTTAWA
TWELVE THOUSAND PERSONS PRESENT
LINCOLN TRIUMPHANT!
VINDICATION OF REPUBLICAN PRINCIPLES!
THE GREAT GIANT SLAIN!

Douglas lost his temper (it was said); Lincoln was in magnificent form and spoke amid cheers. The crowd was three to one for Lincoln. That, of course, was a Republican paper.

The Democrats had a different story:

DOUGLAS AND LINCOLN DEBATE
AT OTTAWA
12,000 PEOPLE WITNESS THE ROUT OF LINCOLN
DOUGLAS AGAIN TRIUMPHANT!

Six days later the debate was at Freeport. Two special trains brought the crowds. Hundreds more came on foot, on horseback, by buggy or wagon. The town was filled with bands, patent medicine hawkers, pickpockets, and devoted followers of one speaker or the other. The crowd flowed through stores, eating houses, and saloons—cleaning up everything. Douglas had come the evening before and was in seclusion at the Brewster Hotel. Lincoln's arrival at nine in the morning was saluted by cannon.

A platform had been built in a nearby grove and at two o'clock the Democrats drove up, with their candidate, in an elegant carriage drawn by handsome white horses. Republicans used a pioneer's Conestoga wagon driven by farmers—no elegance; Lincoln was a man of the people.

The two speakers had very different abilities. Douglas's voice was like organ music, deep and thrilling. Lincoln's was a high tenor which reached to the far edge of the vast crowd. He did not drop his tone at the end of a sentence but kept at an even pitch that held close attention.

There were wide economic and physical differences between the speakers, too. Douglas owned large sections of land in thriving Chicago and in western territories, and he was interested in promoting a railroad between Chicago and the West. Lincoln had only his earnings at law. Douglas was a little over five feet in height and Lincoln six feet and four inches, a contrast that made amusing campaign talk.

"I'm wondering, Mr. Lincoln," a man asked boldly, "how long you figure a man's legs ought to be?"

Lincoln appeared to give the matter thought.

"Well," he decided, "I think to reach from his body to the ground would be about right."

At the Ottawa meeting Douglas had dramatically asked seven questions. Now it was Lincoln's turn to open the debate—and he answered those questions before he began his planned address against Douglas's bill.

This speech, like others he made that summer, was taken down in shorthand by reporters and was published in newspapers over the country. The idea of a debate interested people more than a one-party political rally, and the reports were read by thousands. Three more debates were held in September and two in October.

These debates won national fame for Lincoln. His courage and brilliant logic cut through Douglas's oratory and showed voters one clear issue—should the American people allow slavery to spread? He frankly said he knew no easy way of ending slavery in states where it was legal and that he did not approve of abolition. If slavery could be confined perhaps someday it could be outlawed. But he did know that if slavery spread, the evil would soon be out of control.

Voters over the country pondered words such as these:

"I hate the Kansas-Nebraska bill because of the monstrous injustice of slavery itself. I hate slavery because it deprives our republican example of its just influence in the world.

"Nearly eighty years ago, we began by declaring all men equal. But now" (and he scornfully quoted Douglas) "the 'sacred right of self-government' is the right of one man to enslave the other."

All through the fall, the busy candidates made many other speeches, and men of both parties talked to crowds in towns and villages. Herndon, Trumbull, Browning, Stuart, and others worked hard for the cause and the man they believed in. The battle continued until election day—when Lincoln was defeated.

It took Lincoln several days to get over his chagrin. Eventually, he saw that all was not lost. The intense battle had shown the South that they could not hope to increase the number of slaveholding states, and Douglas had probably lost his chance at the presidency. The Republicans had gained some offices, and Lincoln had won thousands of new friends and supporters. "Old Abe" was now used in a tone of proud affection as well as in the Democratic cartoons, and Mr. Lincoln was being talked of for the presidency in 1860.

During the debates Republican leaders had seen that Lincoln's knowledge of American ideals and history had impressed the people and had gained for him a nation-wide audience. A reputation based on such a foundation might be expected to grow. But if Lincoln thought of this himself, he never let it be known.

After the election of 1858 Lincoln returned to his legal work. While campaigning (at his own expense) his business was neglected, and his income was reduced. Now he worked hard to make up. At home he played with his boys and marketed with the big basket. That winter was very cold, and he took to wearing a woolen shawl twisted around his neck to make a warm muffler. He carried papers in his hat and casually stretched out on the floor whenever he had a few minutes to read.

A visitor at the front door might be met by the man of the house, who had his finger in a book and was hastily settling his coat in place. Mrs. Lincoln, just too late, often hustled to answer his call, "You're wanted, Mother!"

Afterward Mrs. Lincoln scolded. "Mr. Lincoln," she said (a lady did not use her husband's first name), "in your station you should let the girl answer the door!"

Mr. Lincoln grinned—and forgot. Mrs. Lincoln did have her troubles!

In 1859 the people of the United States were increasingly disturbed about slavery. There were riots in Kansas. John Brown attempted to inspire a slave insurrection at Harper's Ferry. And then it came time, in 1860, to nominate a president. The Democrats met first and were so divided that finally southerners chose one candidate and northerners another— Douglas. The remnant of Whigs, now the Constitutional Union Party, had their candidate, too.

Republicans saw that this division of the vote gave them their greatest chance for winning the election. If they nominated the right man, they might elect a president. William Seward, a distinguished easterner, was a general favorite. Illinois, Iowa, and Indiana supported Abraham Lincoln, but he had little other backing. *Harper's Weekly* listed his name seventh among possible candidates: Seward, Bates of

Missouri, and Cameron of Pennsylvania had better chances, *Harper's* said.

Some people thought Lincoln should be present at the Chicago nominating convention, but he did not go. As he had said, "he was a little too much a candidate to stay at home and not quite enough a candidate to go." Many of his friends were going—Judge Davis, Jesse Dubois, Stephen Logan, and William Herndon. They promised to do their best for him and to keep him posted. So Lincoln stayed near the Springfield telegraph office.

On May 14th he received this telegram:

A. LINCOLN: DON'T COME UNLESS WE SEND FOR YOU. DUBOIS AND DAVIS

On the 15th this came:

A. LINCOLN: WE ARE QUIET BUT MOVING HEAVEN AND EARTH. NOTHING WILL BEAT US BUT OLD FOGEY POLITICIANS. THE HEARTS OF THE DELEGATES ARE WITH US. DAVIS AND DUBOIS

On the 18th he had a deluge of messages. The first to bring him the thrilling news was from a friend on the Board of Trade:

ABRAHAM LINCOLN: YOU WERE NOMINATED ON THE 3RD BALLOT. J.J. RICHARDS

His manner was calm, his eyes unrevealing as he looked up and said, "Gentlemen, there is a short little woman at our house who is probably more interested in this dispatch than I am; and if you will excuse me, I will take it up and let her see it." And he went home.

The next morning friends wondered whether he should go to Chicago. But soon a message from the President of the convention settled that problem by telegram:

HON. A. LINCOLN
DEAR SIR: A COMMITTEE OF THE CONVENTION
WILL WAIT UPON YOU BY SPECIAL TRAIN SATURDAY
EVE TO INFORM YOU OFFICIALLY OF YOUR
NOMINATION FOR PRESIDENT OF THE
UNITED STATES.
GEORGE ASHMUN, PRESIDENT

When word got around Springfield that there was to be an official notification, friends hurried to the Lincoln home to advise and help. Lincoln was known to be a "teetotaler"; and he would have nothing in the house suitable to offer distinguished guests.

"I will be glad to take care of everything," a neighbor offered.

"I'll furnish the liquors," another said.

"Gentlemen, I thank you for your kind intentions," Lincoln replied, "but I most respectfully decline your offer. I have no liquors in my house and never have been in the habit of entertaining my friends that way. I cannot permit my friends to do for me what I will not do for myself. I shall provide cold water—nothing else."

Saturday evening a great crowd greeted the two hundred men who came on the special train. Carrying fence rails like muskets they marched to the State House to hear speeches. Then they went to the Lincoln home.

Two boys were waiting for them on the front steps.

"Are you Mr. Lincoln's son?" a visitor asked the older boy. "Yes, sir, I'm Willie," the boy answered briskly.

"Then let's shake!"

"I'm a Lincoln boy, too," seven-year-old Tad spoke up. Laughing, the delegates shook his hand and Tad was happy.

Mr. Lincoln met the committee in the front parlor. His face was quiet and dignified; if he felt pride his gray eyes did not show it. George Ashmun handed him the official letter, and Lincoln bowed as he accepted it.

"I shall reply in writing soon," he said.

"Come up, gentlemen!" someone called out when these formalities were over. "It's nobody but old Abe Lincoln!"

"Mrs. Lincoln will be pleased to see you, gentlemen."

The delegates surged through the house. Mrs. Lincoln was in the south parlor looking pleased and handsome. These Lincolns were not a rough flatboat sort as Easterners half expected. One was heard to remark, "Why, Lincoln's a perfect gentleman!"

Outside, the town blazed with rockets and bonfires. Houses and stores were lighted from basement to attic. Springfield was to be the hub of the country for many a month.

CHAPTER FIFTEEN

PARADES AND FAREWELL

The months between a political nomination and the election give the people their chance to decide how to vote. In 1860, this campaign time promised to be exciting because there were four candidates for President (Southern Democrat, Northern Democrat, Constitutional Union, and Republican). Americans differed widely on the ideas these men represented.

The Republican Party had a three-point platform: to keep slavery out of the territories (but they pledged that it should not be disturbed in states where slaveholding was legal); to protect

Stephen A. Douglas.

American industries; and to give free homestead land to people who wanted to move west.

But these simple phrases displeased many voters. Abolitionists thought them too soft; Southerners read in them an end to slavery. For if slavery could not go along with the movement west, the kind of life dependent upon slavery would surely die out. As for the other points: if factories—mostly in the north—were protected by a high tariff, wealth in the north would rapidly surpass the wealth of the cotton states; and if new land to the west was free, northerners would quickly settle the territories with non-slaveholding people.

The Southern states promptly threatened to withdraw from the Union if the Republican candidate Lincoln was elected. Abolitionists felt that they had been betrayed, and even Republicans were soon frightened. Many regretted Lincoln's nomination. It had seemed a clever move to nominate a "man of the people" like Andrew Jackson; now they wished for the experienced Seward. People of all parties wondered whether it was already too late to keep the states united. The question of leadership must be settled by the people at the election in November.

Party leaders knew that parades draw crowds for the serious speeches and that people value what they work for. So they organized cubs, planned parades and picnics. Ladies—who of course did not vote—sewed the uniforms and made handsome banners. Everyone had a chance to help.

The largest campaign club was the Republican "Wide-Awakes," with more than half a million members by midsummer. Boys formed the "Lincoln Guards" and the

"Young Rail Splitters." Members canvassed voters, escorted speakers, acted as hosts and guides during rallies, and did other valuable service.

While all this was going on, Abraham Lincoln stayed in Springfield, and his days were crowded with duties. He had so many visitors that the governor let him use a pleasant corner room in the State House, and Lincoln held daily receptions there. Artists drew pictures, sculptors made statues, reporters wrote stories, and the campaign committee asked Lincoln to write his own life story.

Willie and Tad Lincoln enjoyed this excitement. They dashed in and out of the State House, bothering everyone but enjoying themselves and entertaining their father. The committee found it hard to be sympathetic when Willie got a mild case of scarlet fever and the fun stopped. Robert, now seventeen, was away finishing his preparation for Harvard University.

Springfield people planned a celebration that should be bigger and better than any in the land. They set the date for August 8th, and everyone went to work. Even opponents agreed to help feed visitors, though announcements warned people to bring their own food if possible. A wigwam designed like the one in Chicago was built near the Square, sidewalks were repaired, extra police appointed, and speakers invited.

August 8th was a clear, hot day, and by nine o'clock the streets were crowded. Special trains brought one hundred and eighty carloads of people, more than fifteen thousand. Thousands and thousands more walked to town or came on horseback, by buggy, or by wagon. They milled around the streets in such numbers that the parade could hardly form. It finally got under way toward Jackson Street, where Mr. Lincoln and his family were to watch it from their front steps.

At the head of the long line was a great ball rolled by uniformed men. Small boys raced alongside trying to read the words on it:

> *Westward the Star of Empire takes its way;*
> *We link-on to Lincoln—our fathers were for Clay.*

Behind the ball marched more than twenty clubs— the "Wide-Awakes," the "Lincoln Young Americans," the "Springfield German-Americans," and others. Bands played, and floats fascinated the crowd. One float was a great flatboat on wheels, marked "New Salem Days." Another had a real power loom that actually made jeans-cloth on the march. As fast as the cloth was woven, lengths were cut off and made into pants "for Lincoln." There was a log-cabin float with a man made up to resemble Lincoln—who split rails all the way. Twenty-three yoke of oxen pulled a huge float carrying rail splitters, wheelwrights, and blacksmiths—who illustrated "honest toil" under the hot sun.

Many marchers carried fence rails. John Hanks had started that fad when Lincoln's name was put in nomination for president at the state convention in May. John had hunted up two of Warnick's rails and had taken them to the convention at Decatur. Delegates were entranced when he pointed out the actual ax marks that "Old Abe" had made. Here were symbols of pioneer toil that people would understand. The idea was so popular that it is a wonder any rail fence was left standing! After Lincoln's nomination thousands and thousands of rails were sold, all supposed to have been split by the Republican candidate. Some of the popular slogans that were tied in with those rails were:

The Union shall be preserved—Old Abe will fence it in.
Abe Lincoln—in Illinois he mauled rails and Stephen A. Douglas.

There were hundreds of gay banners waving snappy slogans in that long, colorful line of march.

By two o'clock the parade had wound back and forth over Springfield streets and arrived at the fair grounds for the speeches. The crowd of some seventy-five thousand was separated into groups where different orators held forth. In the evening there was a torchlight parade. Marching men wore oilcloth capes to protect themselves from sparks and dripping oil. Willie and Tad watched till the last man passed. It was a great day.

The next morning the *Illinois State Journal* carried a glowing account headed by an elephant, the first use of this animal as a campaign symbol. The creature wore two pairs of boots and carried a streamer saying,

"WE ARE COMING!"

On the saddlecloth were the words,

"CLEAR THE TRACK!"

The headlines below the picture said:

A POLITICAL EARTHQUAKE
The prairies on fire for Lincoln!
The Biggest Demonstration Ever Held
in the West

The great rally was but one of many such dramatic gatherings across the country. The vast crowds whipped up strained emotions and kept people conscious of the election—and of their country's political conflict.

The parade was only a brief interruption in Abraham Lincoln's program. The next morning he continued seeing people and reading letters. Market baskets piled with mail arrived daily from the post office, and he attempted to read every letter and to answer (in longhand) as many as he could.

One letter in his daily pile gave him special pleasure.

NY
Westfield Chautauqua Co.
Oct 15, 1860

Hon A B Lincoln
Dear Sir

My father has just come home from the fair and brought home your picture and Mr. Hamlin's. I am a little girl only eleven years old, but want you should be president of the United States very much so I hope you wont think me very bold to write to such a great man as you are. Have you any little girls about as large as I am if so give them my love and tell her to write to me, if you cannot answer this letter. I have got 4 (?) brothers and part of them will vote for you anyway and if you will

*let your whiskers grow I will try and get the rest of them
to vote for you you would look a great deal better for
your face is so thin. All the ladies like whiskers and they
would tease their husbands to vote for you and then you
would be President. My father is agoing to vote for you
to but I will try and get every one to vote for you that
I can think that rail fence around your picture makes it
look very pretty I have got a baby sister she is nine weeks
old and is just as cunning as can be. When you direct
your letter diret to Grace Bedell Westfield Chautauqua
County New York.*

*I must not write any more answer this letter right
off Goodbye*

Grace Bedell

Lincoln replied in his own hand.

Private   *Springfield, Ills.*

Oct. 19, 1860

Miss Grace Bedell

MY DEAR LITTLE MISS,

Your very agreeable letter of the 15th. is received.

*I regret the necessity of saying I have no daughters. I
have three sons—one seventeen, one nine and one seven,
years of age. They, with their mother, constitute my
whole family.*

*As to the whiskers, having never worn any, do you
not think people would call it a piece of silly affection if I
were to begin it now—?*

Your very sincere well-wisher
A. Lincoln

THE PRESIDENTIAL CANDIDATES OF 1860

ABRAHAM LINCOLN became president without even winning a majority of the vote, receiving 1,865,908 votes out of about 4.5 million cast. This was due to the fact that there were four candidates that year:

STEPHEN A. DOUGLAS
The Northern Democratic candidate, also from Illinois, Douglas received almost 1.4 million votes, and might have won the election if not for two other candidates diluting the vote.

It was Douglas's Kansas–Nebraska Act, which sought to allow slavery in some territories where it had been previously closed, that led some Democrats to rebel and form the Republican Party. After losing the election, Douglas became a vigorous supporter of the Union but died of typhoid fever in 1861.

JOHN BRECKINRIDGE
A member of the Southern Democratic Party faction from Kentucky, Breckinridge received 848,000 votes. He was a strong proponent of the rights of states to determine the policy toward slavery. The fact that Northern and Southern Democrats could not agree on a single candidate paved the way for Abraham Lincoln's victory. Breckinridge became a brigadier general and later Secretary of War for the Confederacy.

JOHN BELL
A member of the Constitutional Union Party from Tennessee, Bell initially fought vigorously against secession from the Union and the expansion of slavery but became a strong Confederate advocate.

Pictures taken some weeks after this letter show that Lincoln had grown a beard, in the modish fashion of the day. He wore it the rest of his life. When he went to Washington for his inauguration, the train stopped in Westfield and he met and talked to Grace Bedell.

Election day, November 6th, was clear and warm. Springfield people got up early and milled around the square. Lincoln had decided not to vote; it didn't seem mannerly. But friends told him that his party needed his vote for other offices. So he cut off the upper part of his ticket and voted. Local pride got the better of politics, and men and boys of all parties cheered him when he went to the polls.

When returns began to "tap in," Lincoln went to the small telegraph office and sat tranquilly, awaiting his fate. Reports from the North came first and of course were good. Telegraphers gathered up batches of messages and read news to the people waiting outside. When the South began to be heard from Lincoln remarked, "Now we should get a few licks back!"

At midnight Lincoln and a few others went to a party prepared by the ladies. Mrs. Lincoln, flushed and excited, was there. During the party a few friends risked congratulating Lincoln.

"How do you do, Mr. President?" was a choice bit of wit.

By one-thirty Republican victory seemed certain, and the Lincolns went home. But the city's jollification lasted till

Construction at the U.S. Capitol, including a column named to recognize Abraham Lincoln's election as president on November 6, 1860.

dawn. When the official count was published, Lincoln had won the electoral vote of every free state but New Jersey (it was divided); but his vote was nearly a million less than the total of his opponents, so he was a minority president. And Republicans were a minority in both houses of Congress. It was a staggering task that awaited him in Washington—made worse by the fact that many, both Republicans and Democrats, thought that Lincoln's election was a national calamity. Now when it was too late, many Republicans wished that the experienced Seward had been elected; Democrats saw in Lincoln's election the end of the union of states and probably civil war. Meanwhile, Buchanan, with the best of intention and little forcefulness, marked time in Washington. Everyone waited as people wait for a burning fuse to set off a bomb.

In preparation for his new office Lincoln must select his cabinet and write his inaugural address. But how was a man to think and write when the country seemed to be going to pieces around him? Soon after the election South Carolina seceded. Every mail brought word of more trouble! Southerners honestly believed that only by withdrawing from the Union could they save their way of life. Soon six other states— Georgia, Alabama, Mississippi, Louisiana, Florida, and Texas—joined South Carolina and formed the Confederate States of America with the distinguished Jefferson Davis, former United States Senator, as their president.

In December, frightened statesmen tried to get some agreement that would save the country. They even proposed that the Missouri Compromise be restored. But Lincoln refused because he had been elected on his promise that slavery should not spread. It was too late to bring back an agreement that would let slavery into the west.

Terror—a secret, fearful terror—spread like a sickness over the country. Even Republicans who had voted for Lincoln felt that they had gone too far. Many were relieved when word got out that William Seward was to be the Secretary of State. He was a "safe man." He could save the country. Lincoln, they now thought, didn't know much about statecraft.

In the midst of all this turmoil, Lincoln gathered a few books and shut himself in a back room over a store to write his address. He had with him his history of the United States with the Declaration of Independence and the Constitution, the speeches of his favorite statesmen—Webster, Jackson, and Clay—and the Bible. The country eyed that room. What was Lincoln writing? Would he try to appease and save the nation from war? Or would he defy—and bring on armed conflict?

In February, after the Confederates had taken several Gulf forts and had threatened Fort Sumter, the speech was finished. The cabinet was chosen too: Lincoln asked his three rivals for the nomination—Seward, Bates, and Cameron—and four others to be his advisers. This must have taken courage, but Lincoln never lacked for that.

Now it was time to wind up personal business in Springfield. He rented his house and sold the furniture. He traveled to Charleston, Illinois, to bid his stepmother good-bye and see that she was well cared for. He had a long talk with Billy Herndon about their law partnership; and as he left the office, he pointed to their shabby sign.

"Let it hang," he said. "Give our clients to understand that the election of a president makes no change in the firm of Lincoln & Herndon. If I live, I'm coming back sometime; and then we'll go right on practicing law as if nothing had ever happened."

He went to Billy's Barber Shop and had the new beard trimmed. Proud Billy hated to see his friend go away.

"We colored people will miss you, Mr. Lincoln," he said.

After Lincoln left the shop, Billy remarked to a friend: "I feel uneasy about Mr. Lincoln—almost as though he may never come back to Springfield." Billy stood at the window watching as Lincoln walked away.

Long ago Abe Lincoln had felt a clear conviction about the time to leave New Salem. His success in law and in politics had proved the rightness of that decision. But leaving Springfield seemed hardly an act of his own choosing. He was now riding a tide of monstrous events.

The eleventh of February was a dreary day. Mr. Lincoln drove to the railroad station in a drizzle of cold rain. But weather did not keep friends from coming to see him off. The crowds made it impossible to say a personal farewell to each one, but he could not leave without expressing his friendship. After he got aboard the train he walked through to the end platform and stood a moment in the cold, looking at these loyal friends. Then he spoke to them:

"My friends: No one, not in my situation, can appreciate my feeling of sadness at this parting. To this place, and the kindness of these people, I owe everything. Here I have lived a quarter of a century, and have passed from a young to an old man. Here my children have been born, and one is buried. I now leave, not knowing when or whether ever, I may return, with a task before me greater than that which rested upon Washington. Without the assistance of that Divine Being, who ever attended him, I cannot succeed. With that assistance I cannot fail. Trusting in Him who can go with me, and remain with you, and be every where for good, let us confidently hope that all will yet be well. To His care commending you, as I hope in your prayers you will commend me, I bid you an affectionate farewell."

Lincoln turned, pulled his old gray shawl tighter around his neck, and went into the car. The whistle blew. The train stirred; people waited as it slowly moved out of sight. Then they silently turned away. Abraham Lincoln, their friend and neighbor, was gone from their town. Uneasy and sad, they plodded to their homes.

CHAPTER SIXTEEN

WASHINGTON IN 1861

The journey from Springfield to Washington could be done in two or three days, but Lincoln's trip was to last two weeks. The train was to stop at many places where he would see important people, hold conferences, and make speeches. His advisers hoped that a sight of him might quiet rising tension. His manner was so friendly that shaking his hand made a person feel his kindly nature and gave people confidence.

So it was the twenty-first of February when he arrived in Philadelphia. Mrs. Lincoln and the small boys had joined him, and they were conducted from train to hotel with a great parade.

The inauguration of Abraham Lincoln, March 4, 1861.

Few knew that while gay crowds thronged the streets three men were anxiously conferring in a small room. Two were friends of Lincoln who were making the trip with him. The third was the detective, Allan Pinkerton.

"There is a plot to murder Mr. Lincoln in Baltimore!" Pinkerton told them.

The men were not so surprised as Pinkerton had expected. They knew Lincoln's life had been threatened; likely this was just another crackpot. Lincoln would laugh at their fears. But the detective was insistent. Vague threats could be brushed off. This was a definite plot. Lincoln must not go through Baltimore by daylight, as planned.

"Then you'll have to tell him yourself!" the men said.

Pinkerton went to Lincoln that evening and was laughed at for his worry. Lincoln had planned to attend a flag-raising at Independence Hall, Philadelphia, the next day, to speak in Harrisburg, and to go through Baltimore; and he intended to carry out that plan. After much argument he was persuaded to protect himself by letting them slip him through Baltimore in the night. But he refused to miss that ceremony at Independence Hall and the speech at Harrisburg.

The next day the flag was raised, and Mr. Lincoln spoke words that showed his deep love for the famous document written in that hall.

"I am filled with deep emotion (he said) at finding myself standing . . . in this place . . . from which sprang the institutions under which we live. . . . All the political sentiments I entertain have been drawn . . . from sentiments

which originated and were given to the world from this hall."
He said that he thought often of the men who wrote the
Declaration of Independence and the army that achieved the
freedom it declared. Liberty should not be just for separation
from the mother country; it should be for all people in the
world for all future time. If the country could be saved with
freedom for all, he would be the happiest of men. If it could
not be saved with freedom, "I would rather be assassinated
on this spot than surrender it." And he promised that there
would be no blood shed except in self-defence.

After he had finished in Philadelphia and Harrisburg, he
reluctantly allowed himself to be smuggled through Baltimore
in the night. But when he arrived safely in Washington the
next morning, he said it was a shabby way to approach the
greatest office in the land.

Hours behind him, the special train with his family and
party arrived in Washington, and they joined him at the
Willard Hotel. At once the Lincoln suite took on the gay air
of a continual party. Mrs. Lincoln had pretty sisters, nieces,
and cousins with her and handsome Robert had come down
from Harvard for his father's inauguration. Mr. Lincoln's two
secretaries were attractive young men and had their hands
full managing the many visitors.

Robert was a mannerly youth. His middle name Todd
was aptly chosen, for he was a Kentucky gentleman—and
always correct. Willie and Tad gleefully dodged through the
rooms; they were by now badly pampered youngsters, but
their devoted father seemed to find their energy diverting.

And so the important day drew near.

March 4th was windy and raw in spite of sunshine. Thousands who had come to see the inauguration could not find places to sleep. They washed at public fountains and milled around the city. A few buildings were gaily decorated. Others were tightly shuttered, reminding visitors that Washington, like Baltimore, was really a southern city. Pennsylvania Avenue had been freshly swept and looked its best, but the sight of Federal soldiers marching to stations along the way was disturbing. Sabers gleamed; feet tramped with military correctness. The crowds eyed the soldiers uncomfortably.

Many friends had come from Illinois for the day. Among these was Mentor Graham, the kindly schoolteacher of New Salem. He had drawn from his precious savings: bought a new suit, hat, and railroad ticket. This day, when the youth he had taught grammar and surveying would become the president of the United States, was a great day in Graham's life.

As Abraham Lincoln stepped onto the platform, he was carefully dressed. His suit was well made, his tall hat shone, his shirt bosom was white, his boots new, and he carried a shiny ebony cane topped with gold. But where should he put the thing? The small stand before him would barely hold the manuscript of his address.

Senator Douglas, sitting near, reached out, took both hat and cane, and held them through the ceremony. Mr. Lincoln gazed at the assembled people; many a time he and Douglas had faced as big a crowd on a prairie. How strange to be together here; one holding a hat, one taking a high office.

Senator Baker of Oregon made the introduction. "Fellow citizens, I introduce to you Abraham Lincoln, the President-elect of the United States."

Hardly a ripple of applause broke the tense silence as Mr. Lincoln stepped to the speaker's stand, took his address from his pocket, and began to speak.

"Fellow citizens of the United States: In compliance with a custom as old as the government itself, I appear before you to address you briefly, and to take in your presence, the oath prescribed by the Constitution of the United States, to be taken by the President 'before he enters on the execution of his office.'"

Then in clear statements he assured Southern states that he would not interfere with slavery where it was legal and that fugitive slaves from such states would be returned. He reminded the South that forts belonged to the Federal government, but that he would try to avoid irritation in carrying out government work. These matters attended to, he began what to him was the most important part of his address: he begged the people to keep an unbroken union.

"Physically . . . we cannot separate," he said. "We cannot remove our respective sections one from each other, nor build an impassable wall between. . . . Suppose you go to war, you cannot fight always; and when, after much loss on both sides and no gain on either you cease fighting, the identical old questions . . . are again upon you. . . . Nothing valuable can be lost by taking time . . . Intelligence, patriotism, Christianity,

A copy of the Emancipation Proclamation.

and a firm reliance on Him who has never yet forsaken this favored land, are still competent to adjust in the best way all our present difficulty. . . .

"I am loathe to close. We are not enemies but friends. We must not be enemies. Though passion may have strained, it must not break our bonds of affection. The mystic chords of memory, stretching from every battlefield and patriot grave to every living heart and hearthstone all over this broad land will yet swell the chorus of the Union when again touched, as surely they will be, by the better angels of our nature."

The high, clear voice stopped. Chief Justice Taney opened the Bible. Lincoln raised his right hand and repeated after the justice the solemn oath, "I do solemnly swear that I will faithfully execute the office of President of the United States and will, to the best of my ability, preserve, protect, and defend the Constitution of the United States."

Guns boomed. The crowd stirred. In this crucial moment of the country's existence, Abraham Lincoln was now the President of the United States.

That evening the Lincolns attended the "Union Ball," and the next morning Mr. Lincoln began his enormous task as chief executive. He held cabinet meetings at which he tried to get his new "team" working. He saw hundreds of office seekers. They flocked to the White House, entered unquestioned, and stood in line on the stairs leading to his office. The Lincolns had no privacy at all!

Washington ladies gossiped about Mrs. Lincoln, her high-handed ways of starting housekeeping, and her gowns;

Robert Lincoln went back to college; and Willie and Tad got sick. This time it was the measles.

Mrs. Lincoln was eager to take her proper place as "First Lady" and also to show that her native Kentucky was not the backwoods that many called it; so when the boys were well she began official entertaining. This, considering her husband's casual ideas, presented difficulties.

There was even the matter of dress, especially gloves. By the third reception she had got him into a pair of white gloves—quite an achievement as his hands were large and muscular from grasping an ax most of his growing years. But all went well—until the President spied an old friend from Sangamon County coming down the line. He reached out and grasped the neighbor's hand and—pop! That glove burst like an inflated paper bag.

Elegant guests stared. Mr. Lincoln inspected the shattered glove and remarked, "Well, my friend, that was quite a bustification." And the party went on.

As it turned out, fate did not allow time for the calm thinking that Mr. Lincoln had begged for in his speech. On March 5th, the day after he was inaugurated, Lincoln was shown a letter from Major Anderson, the commander of Fort Sumter, in the harbor at Charleston, South Carolina. The major wrote that his provisions would soon be gone and that twenty thousand men were needed to hold that fort. He had less than a hundred and asked if he should withdraw. The new cabinet disagreed about what to do.

Before any action was decided on, three agents of the new Confederate government arrived in Washington to ask for recognition of their independence, and to settle the matter of forts and property in the South.

Secretary Seward wangled delay and tried to conciliate everyone. The agents thought Sumter was going to be evacuated, so they stayed on in Washington. While Seward bustled about, Lincoln decided that now was the time to show the authority of the Union. Against the advice of members of his cabinet, he ordered help sent to the fort. He thought that delay would allow the Confederacy to grow stronger, perhaps so strong that it could not be overthrown. And as for the North, delay might cool union sentiment so that the country could never be brought together.

The Southern agents went home and on April 12, Confederate guns fired on Fort Sumter.

Three days later President Lincoln called for 75,000 volunteers and three weeks later for 42,000 more. By the first of July he had 310,000 under arms. The ships of the Navy were called home and Southern ports were blockaded.

The South, too, acted quickly. Jefferson Davis called for 100,000 volunteers; and four more states, Arkansas, Virginia, North Carolina, and Tennessee joined the Confederacy. Maryland, Kentucky, and Missouri hesitated.

And so began a civil war, the most dreadful of all wars because it sets family against family. Lincoln's own people were divided as were many others; he had relatives who chose to fight for the South; three of Mrs. Lincoln's brothers enlisted in the Confederate Army. Many hardly knew which side to support; Robert E. Lee and George H. Thomas were both West Point graduates and citizens of Virginia and were torn between conflicting loyalties. Lee decided he could not fight against his home and family; Thomas decided to fight for the Union and served with distinction under General Grant.

On the surface the war was to settle two questions: Should slavery be extended? Did states that had entered the Union have the right to withdraw from it? But Mr. Lincoln and other thoughtful men knew that deep down under those questions lay another, even more important: Could a government founded on the principles of the Declaration of Independence survive?

Soon the line of office seekers was replaced by a longer line of men who wanted commissions in the army or the chance to tell the President how to run the country. Everyone thought he knew just what should be done. Few, even in his own cabinet, had faith in Lincoln's ability. Seward thought of Lincoln as a mere puppet and of himself as the real leader of the government. The cabinet debated the merits of various generals; the shocking defeat at the Battle of Bull Run in July showed they needed competent men, but who were they?

Mr. Lincoln had little time for rest or recreation except stolen moments with his family. Willie and Tad got up a show in the attic, had a menagerie back of the house, and gave circus performances with goats, birds, ponies, and other creatures given to them. Wide-eyed youngsters peered through the fence and were invited in for the fun. The Lincoln boys (Willie was eleven and Tad eight) were used to picking friends as they pleased; they cared nothing whether a lad was a son of wealth or poverty; if he wanted to come, he was invited in. When work piled up, the President liked to leave his desk and see what his boys were doing. A laugh at their antics refreshed him.

Mrs. Lincoln was a devoted mother and was never too busy to make sure her boys were well and happy. She had reluctantly consented that Willie be allowed to ride his pony. This pretty animal was Willie's most prized gift, and he rode daily.

One cold winter afternoon he came in wet and chilled. His mother put him to bed, but he did not sleep off the illness as she had hoped; so a doctor was called.

The next evening there was to be a formal reception at the White House; but Dr. Stone thought Willie would be all right, so the party was not cancelled. Both the President and Mrs. Lincoln came upstairs often that evening to make sure the sick child was sleeping. Alas! Willie got steadily worse, and he died a few days later.

Mr. Lincoln was crushed with grief. "My poor boy! God has called him home," he cried. Mrs. Lincoln was so overcome that Mr. Lincoln feared for her health. Little Tad was lost without his brother. He often ran into his father's office and threw his arms about the man, hugging tight. Then he ran back to lonely play or stayed by his father to nap. Visitors saw the President leave his office and carry a sleeping little boy to bed. The White House seemed different after Willie died.

Perhaps because war began at once, the President and Mrs. Lincoln who had made few intimate friends in Washington. Now their greatest help came from Mrs. Elizabeth Keckley, a kindly dressmaker to Mrs. Lincoln who had become a friend.

In these sad days the President came to depend on her. He loved all his boys, but Willie was "the Lincoln," the one most like his father. Mrs. Lincoln grieved for many months when her husband needed her gaiety and her faith in him.

The war was going badly in that year 1862. The President began to wonder if the Union could possibly be saved while slaves were still in bondage. Years before he had proposed that the government purchase and free slaves but the suggestion was talked down as "too expensive." (Years later historians figured that the Civil War cost more than twice as much as buying and freeing the slaves.) At the time he made the suggestion he could not enforce it. Now with war powers given to the President he could free slaves in rebellious states. How should it be done? For months he studied this problem.

In the summer of 1862, when General McClellan was building a fine army but not winning battles, the President went to the telegraph office and sat at a desk to write. Here, in the midst of tapping instruments, he was free from seekers and complainers. Presently he wrote a few words, locked the paper in a drawer, and went away. But he came again, and again. Sometimes he wrote half a page; sometimes he only changed what he had written before. Men watched him and said nothing. They saw he was trying to put deep thoughts into words.

In July, Lincoln talked with Seward and Gideon Welles, the Secretary of the Navy, about the emancipation of the slaves. They were astonished at the change in his thinking and begged for time to consider before giving an opinion.

Early in August the President called a cabinet meeting and laid the matter before them. Many objections were made but as he had foreseen most of these, Lincoln had an answer ready for each one. Seward alone had an idea that Lincoln had not considered. He suggested that the matter wait until a Union victory put the country in a mood favorable for change. To this Lincoln agreed.

Meanwhile Abolitionists prodded the President to take a decisive stand and free the slaves. Delegations came to the White House to plead; many wrote vigorous letters. On the 19th of August, Horace Greeley of the *New York Tribune* published an open letter to Lincoln in which he reproved the President for delay and demanded that he confiscate and free the slaves at once. Greeley claimed that he expressed the views of twenty million people.

Lincoln's answer to Greeley's criticism of his policy was prompt and clear. ". . . I would save the Union the shortest way under the Constitution. . . . If there be those who would not save the Union unless they could at the same time save slavery, I do not agree with them. If there be those who would not save the Union unless they could at the same time destroy slavery, I do not agree with them. My paramount object in this struggle is to save the Union. . . .

"I have here stated my purpose according to my view of official duty; and I intend no modification of my oft expressed personal wish that all men everywhere could be free."

And he continued to wait for the right moment.

But after the Union victory at Antietam, Lincoln could wait no longer. That inward force that often guided him made him sure that the time had come to speak. He called a cabinet meeting on the 22nd of September.

"I made a promise to myself," he told the assembled secretaries, "and to my Maker. I am going to fulfill that promise now." And he read to them the fateful words he had written in the proclamation to free the slaves.

The message warned the states and parts of states that were "in rebellion against the United States" and said that "unless they ceased war against the government . . . persons held as slaves within . . . such states . . . are henceforth and forever free . . . and the government of the United States . . . will recognize and maintain the freedom of said persons."

He asked "freed persons" to refrain from violence and to work for fair wages, and he promised them work in forts and on ships. This, he read, was an act of justice and was legal, and he begged the considerate judgment of men and the favor of God. If signed, the proclamation was to be effective January 1, 1863.

Many times Lincoln's cabinet had disagreed with him. That day they approved the proclamation and it was promptly signed.

This famous document declared free only the slaves in states which had withdrawn from the Union, so it actually had relatively little effect upon the total number of slaves. But its moral value was enormous. Northerners saw in it a sign that Lincoln truly did hope to free the slaves. While Abolitionists thought it far too mild, they admitted it was a good first step toward the right goal.

In Europe, and especially in England, sentiment for the South had been growing; now, when they saw Lincoln's stand, plans for intervention were laid aside and liberals turned to Lincoln's support.

Many regarded Emancipation, limited as it was, as the most important step in man's march for freedom since the Declaration of Independence in 1776.

But its effect on the war was to intensify feeling. The North now had a moral crusade; the South, a fight for life.

CHAPTER SEVENTEEN

THE MIDDLE WAR YEARS

In the fall of 1862, the President made a visit to the Army of the Potomac. He wanted to see this army and to talk personally with its general. McClellan had won at Antietam with a terrible cost in men, but he was not following up this advantage. Perhaps the general was better fitted for organizing than for fighting. Alas! A war is not won by soldiers sitting in a well-run camp.

Lincoln made his inspection on horseback. He was an easy rider and rode more gracefully than he walked. He had the conference with McClellan, who was determined to follow his own plans.

President Lincoln and General McClellan.

"Are you not overcautious when you assume that you cannot do what the enemy is constantly doing?" Lincoln asked him. But McClellan had excuses for postponing battle.

So, after he returned to Washington, the President gave McClellan other work and appointed Major General Burnside in charge of the Army of the Potomac. Now, he hoped, he would get action.

But Burnside disappointed his chief. After one battle Lincoln replaced him with "Fighting Joe" Hooker, and in the spring of '63 went again to visit the army.

This time Mrs. Lincoln and Tad went with the President. Mrs. Lincoln was not well, and Lincoln thought this trip would divert her. Tad loved it, and the men liked him. They gave him a horse, and an orderly rode with him. At the official review Tad galloped alongside the cavalry, his gray cloak flying, his eyes sparkling.

After the review the President visited with men in the hospital tents. He strolled from cot to cot, taking time to talk with each man.

"Did you hear what's said about the review," a whisper followed the tall visitor. "The President touched his hat to the officers, correctly, but he took it clear off to the men!"

"There's a man for me!" men said, and they cheered him when he left for headquarters.

This visit encouraged the President. Mighty guns, great cavalry troops, thousands of trained men should bring the war to an end soon. But Hooker was overconfident, Lincoln thought. The Commander in Chief was still uneasy about his general.

Other important matters were on his mind, too. He sponsored many changes that were for the country's welfare—changes that people engrossed in war hardly noticed or credited to him.

He proclaimed the last Thursday in November as a day of national Thanksgiving, and through the Treasury Department, he had the words, "In God We Trust," put on coins. These words were first used on a two-cent piece and then on many coins. (The first time the phrase was used on a penny was the "Lincoln Penny" of 1909.)

Perhaps Lincoln remembered the confusion in postage rates back in New Salem when he signed the order for a uniform rate of postage in the United States. In July, 1863, free delivery of mail in forty-nine cities was begun. During the war years the first post-office cars were used on railroads and the first railway labor union was organized.

The Civil War was the first "railroad war" and army men were astonished to find they could not use all the roads. Each different railroad company had its own width of track, and cars could not be switched from one road to the other. Early railroad builders had adopted George Stephenson's English gauge, with the tracks four feet and eight and a half inches apart. Newer roads chose other widths, independent of each other, four feet to five feet wide.

When the Union Pacific Railroad was charted in 1862, the company asked Mr. Lincoln to choose a point where the line should begin in Nebraska (he picked Omaha) and to select a gauge. In the midst of war duties he took time to study gauges and decided on the four-foot, eight-and-a-half-inch width. Other railroads noticing that he gave the gauge so much attention, adopted the width he selected; and so, for the first time, cars and engines could be switched from road to road and transcontinental travel became possible.

The opening up of the West turned people's thinking to agriculture and a Department of Agriculture was started in Lincoln's second year of office.

Foreign affairs were not neglected either. The President recognized the governments of Haiti and Liberia and developed the friendship with Russia which made it possible for the United States to buy Alaska five years later.

He took time to write a tactful letter to the King of Siam. The King had sent gifts of elephants' tusks and pictures of himself and his daughter and had offered to send pairs of elephants for setting up herds in the United States. The intent was appreciated and Lincoln's refusal must surely be the most diplomatic "No!" ever written. These are, in part, his words:

"I appreciate most highly your Majesty's tender of good offices. Our political jurisdiction, however, does not reach a latitude so low as to favor the multiplication of the elephant, and steam on land as well as on the water has been our best and most efficient agent of transportation in internal commerce. . . ."

Inventors of war weapons heard that the President would receive and study new ideas; so many came to the White House. Some of their ideas and claims were ridiculous. But the President had kindly ways of managing them.

One man came away chuckling. "You should hear the riddle the President told me," he remarked to a friend.

" 'Suppose I call a sheep's tail a leg,' he said to me; 'then how many legs has a sheep?'

" 'Five,' I said.

" 'Not so,' the President corrected. 'A sheep has four legs. Calling a tail a leg doesn't make it one.' You have to really show that man—telling isn't enough."

Time spent with inventors got results. Lincoln approved experimental use of several kinds of weapons. Use of balloons for observation was begun in the summer of 1861. He ordered three "ironclads" after he saw the plans for Ericsson's *Monitor*, a new type of ship with an iron-covered hull.

There were other "firsts" too. The first draft law was passed, the first Congressional Medal of Honor was awarded, and for the first time soldiers on duty away from home were allowed to vote. Both military police and army medical care were started.

The President must have rejoiced when the Kansas-Nebraska Act was repealed and when new laws opening free homestead lands and setting up a national banking system settled business problems that were debated in his youth.

And all the time Lincoln continued his search for competent generals. The South had a brilliant leader in the West Point–trained General Robert E. Lee; had the North no one his equal? Daily the President had to hear bitter criticism of his conduct of the war—all the harder to bear because he was earnestly trying to win in the shortest possible time. Lincoln well knew that until the war was won he could not announce his cherished plans for strengthening the Union. In his despair he sometimes wondered whether the form of government undertaken in the United States was a noble dream for which the world was not yet ready.

At night the President walked the floor of the silent White House. The misery of thousands was his own grief, for since Willie's death he knew what it was to see a tall son die. Perhaps Willie would be alive today if his father had stayed in Springfield! The tenderhearted "Abe" Lincoln who could not shoot wild turkeys must now send thousands of fine men to battle. It seemed sometimes that he could not endure to stand by and see soldiers court-martialed and shot for sleeping at post of duty when they were exhausted—yet he knew discipline was necessary. At times the President seemed overwhelmed by the misery of civil war.

Often his pacing ended on his knees, begging God for help and guidance. God seemed nearer, somehow, since Willie was gone. Willie's lonely father prayed to find God's way and for the strength to follow it. And so long nights passed and each day the problems of war mounted.

War news was usually about movements in the East. People talked about "taking Richmond" and "defending Washington." Few noticed what the Navy was doing on the Mississippi River or complained to the President that no general had taken that Gibraltar of the river, the fort at Vicksburg, Mississippi. As for Ulysses S. Grant, a West Point graduate, people hardly noticed when he re-entered the army and was sent to serve in the midwest. But Grant was not seeking fame for himself. He was busy planning how to take Vicksburg. It would not easily be won.

In the spring of 1863, after an uncomfortable, disappointing winter of effort that ended in failure, Grant made a bold plan. With his men he crossed the river from the west and camped south of Vicksburg. At the same time the United States Navy ran the gauntlet of river forts to join him. There, in June, Grant boldly besieged the city. His plans were so well laid and carried out that on July 4th Vicksburg surrendered and on the 9th a Federal steamboat traveled from St. Louis to New Orleans without interference.

But news of this success was slow in reaching the East because a messenger had to take it 600 twisting miles by steamboat to Cairo before it could be put on the wires!

During the weeks when Grant was quietly maneuvering near Vicksburg, General Hooker of the Army of the Potomac suffered a bitter defeat at Chancellorsville. Lee's Confederate army, hoping now to gain a quick victory, moved north—perhaps to raid the rich Shenandoah Valley, perhaps to attack Washington. Hooker cut across to defend the capital. Spies from both armies were cut off and neither knew, at that critical end of June, just where the opposing army was located.

In this crisis, Hooker was refused more troops and resigned his command. The President, smarting under criticism of Hooker's recent defeat, ordered George Meade, an officer on Hooker's staff, to take his place.

Meade was a good army man, safe rather than brilliant, but he had never planned a battle. Sixty regiments of his army had left for home, their enlistment time ended. In their place, he had thousands of new, untrained recruits. Lee's army was thought to be near, but Meade, in desperation, wondered where?

Four days after Meade got his orders, a few of his men literally stumbled onto Lee's army and a major battle at Gettysburg, Pennsylvania, began. The fierce fighting lasted three days; the slaughter was shocking. On the evening of July 4th, Lee gathered what little was left of his army and slipped away. He knew that hope for victory that summer was ended. Efforts to make peace with a recognition of the Confederacy would be futile.

Meade and the remnant of his army were too exhausted to realize at once that they had won a great victory.

These two major victories, coming actually on the same day, effectively turned the tide of war. Nearly two years were to pass before the war ended, but after July 4, 1863, there was little question as to which army would ultimately win.

Weeks after that fateful July day, someone suggested that the government buy land at Gettysburg for a national cemetery. Popular sentiment approved. An October day was set for the dedication and the greatest living orator, Honorable Edward Everett, was asked to make the address. He replied that he needed time to prepare his speech; so the date was changed to November.

No one suggested that the President speak. The committee wanted an orator who could do justice to this solemn occasion. As an afterthought someone asked Mr. Lincoln to say a few words. "Just say something to set apart formally these grounds to their sacred use," the President was told.

Abraham Lincoln accepted and began turning over in his mind what he should say. It must be short—was this the time and place to speak his thoughts about government and the Union? He began to set on paper words to express his exact meaning.

Late in the evening of November 17th, William Slade, the steward at the White House, came to the President's study to see if anything was needed before he went off duty. The steward was a free black man from Virginia. His business was buying food used in the White House, catering for parties, and such work. The President liked him and trusted him; Slade had become Mr. Lincoln's confidential messenger, a kind of valet and personal friend. Lincoln valued Slade as Mrs. Lincoln cherished the friendship of Mrs. Keckley. Now he wanted Slade's help.

"Listen to this, William," Mr. Lincoln said, "See how you think it sounds." He read aloud the talk he had written for the dedication.

"I like it, Mr. President," Slade said. "It's good."

Reassured Lincoln went to bed.

The next day the President and a large party went from Washington to Gettysburg by special train. In his pocket he had the paper he had read to William Slade. On the train he took it out to make a slight change. Men nearby saw him writing and thought that he had carelessly left writing his speech until this last minute.

On the 19th the parade formed and marched to the cemetery. Notables sat on a wooden platform and grew bored during the long, long prayer and Everett's two-hour address. When the President was introduced he seemed just one speaker too many.

He stepped forward, his kindly eyes on the cold, weary people. His words were spoken in slow, clear tones, easy to follow:

"Four score and seven years ago our fathers brought forth on this continent, a new nation, conceived in Liberty, and dedicated to the proposition that all men are created equal.

"Now we are engaged in a great civil war, testing whether that nation, or any nation so conceived and so dedicated, can long endure. We are met on a great battlefield of that war. We have come to dedicate a portion of that field, as a final resting place for those who here gave their lives that the nation might live. It is altogether fitting and proper that we should do this.

"But, in a larger sense, we cannot dedicate—we cannot consecrate—we cannot hallow—this ground. The brave men, living and dead, who struggled here, have consecrated it, far above our poor power to add or detract. The world will little note, nor long remember what we say here, but it can never forget what they did here. It is for us the living, rather, to be dedicated here to the unfinished work which they who fought here have thus far so nobly advanced. It is rather for us to be dedicated here to the great task remaining before us—that from those honored dead we take increased devotion to that cause for which they gave the last full measure of devotion— that we here highly resolve that those dead shall not have died in vain—that this nation, under God, shall have a new birth of freedom—and that government of the people, by the people, for the people, shall not perish from the earth."

The echo of his last word faded. There was little applause. As he turned to his seat Lincoln felt that his speech had failed to express his ideals to the people. The crowd broke up and hurried home.

When people read the speech in the newspapers the next day they thrilled with Lincoln's noble conception of the purpose of the war. They gained a truer understanding of his high hope for the Union. But it was for later generations to realize that the Gettysburg Address was a literary masterpiece. The world had found in it inspiration to strive for the ideal of government Abraham Lincoln had so eloquently expressed.

• CHAPTER EIGHTEEN •

"WITH MALICE TOWARD NONE"

The glow of victories continued through the autumn months. Grant and Meade were heroes of the time. The President's skill in keeping Kentucky from seceding was little noticed. Few realized that he had kept Missouri as a safety zone, or observed the important work the Navy was doing on the Mississippi River. Lincoln rejoiced in the sense of winning, and he too now felt sure that he had found the right generals.

"The Lord is on our side!" someone remarked and Lincoln answered quickly:

General Ulysses S. Grant.

"I am not so much concerned that the Lord should be on our side," he said. "I pray daily that we may be on the Lord's side."

Grant followed up his success at Vicksburg with a victory at Chattanooga in November; so early in 1864 the President gave him command of all the Union armies. Congress approved, and revived the rank of Lieutenant General which George Washington had held. Grant was voted this honor and ordered to Washington.

On the eighth of March (1864) the President and Mrs. Lincoln were giving a reception and word got around that Grant might be there. The rooms were crowded with guests.

Grant had not expected a party. As he left the train, travelworn and wearing his service uniform, he went directly to the White House.

The Executive Mansion was brightly lighted, but Grant hardly noticed. He asked to see the President, and was ushered into the crowded rooms. Often the measure of a man's greatness is shown in such a time. Grant walked forward. A few recognized him from his pictures and drew back, respectfully. Chatter stopped. Grant reached the room where the President was receiving, and the two great men faced each other. They needed no introduction. The short, shabby soldier looked up at the tall gaunt President, and they clasped hands.

Secretary Seward, ever ready to do the correct thing, introduced the general to Mrs. Lincoln. Guests, recovering breath, cheered till the crystal drops on the chandeliers tinkled. Crowds surged near to shake the general's hand. Seward edged him to a sofa—from it General Grant spoke briefly, and then met the long line of guests.

The next morning Grant came again to the White House and his commission as Lieutenant General was formally presented. The President made a short speech, a part of which was:

" . . . As the country herein trusts you, so, under God, it will sustain you. . . . with what I speak here for the nation goes my own hearty personal concurrence."

Now people were hopeful. Few guessed then that a year of fighting was still ahead.

President Lincoln's popularity went up and down along with the success of battles. Through the middle of his term he seemed to have more enemies than friends. But after Grant took command that changed.

In June a convention met in Baltimore to nominate a president. Most men attending were Republicans; but since there were also some who called themselves "War Democrats," the convention was named the "National Union" convention.

Mr. Lincoln must have chuckled when he heard what happened there. Now, after the months of bitter criticism, men actually fought for the honor of nominating him for president! He won on the first ballot.

But popularity is a fragile thing. By August, when the city of Washington was threatened and the rebel army was in sight of the Capitol itself, it seemed that Lincoln could not possibly be elected. He himself did not expect it. That midsummer raid did not succeed, but it hurt people's faith in the Union. Even Grant slipped from his pedestal, and the mournful song, "We're Tenting Tonight," was heard more often than the "Battle Hymn of the Republic."

But the autumn successes of Farragut, Grant, and Sherman changed everything again, and Lincoln won the election.

"If I know my heart," Lincoln said when he was congratulated, "my gratitude is free from any taint of personal triumph."

Thoughtful voters may have been surprised when they learned that Lincoln was elected by a large majority although he was in disagreement with the Congress (which was elected then too) on the next most important problem—what to do with the South after the war. His triumph was clearly a personal victory; was it also a vote of confidence for his determination to consider rebellious states as still members of the Union? Only time would answer that question.

And now Abraham Lincoln prepared for another inauguration. The war seemed to be ending. His thoughts were about how to unite a nation of brothers who had been enemies. No one knew just what Lincoln had in his mind to do. But all knew that he wished for justice, tempered with mercy.

"We must not sully victory with harshness," was an idea he often expressed. But paying Southerners for slaves and softening defeat with kindness were not popular ideas around the President. It was a hard winter, with need every day to watch his words.

Lincoln aged rapidly during this time. He had little recreation to balance his responsibilities. Parties were stiff, formal affairs—no rest for a weary man. Summers, the Lincolns lived in a cottage at the Soldiers' Home outside of Washington, and the President enjoyed the trips to and from his office. Winters, he was much confined.

Washington life had been disappointing to Mrs. Lincoln. She was an ambitious woman, and the bitter criticism of the President and herself had been hard to endure. Like many others she had family ties on both sides of the fighting. That strain, Willie's death, and her own difficult nature made her draw into herself.

The one amusement which both Mr. and Mrs. Lincoln enjoyed in the winter was the theater. They attended whenever a Shakespearean play or other good bill was shown. The marshal at the White House worried about Lincoln's safety. The President had no fear! He would walk around the city, drive to the country, or sit in an open box at the theater— how could they guard a man like that? But Lincoln went his way, unafraid. And March came.

The rain dripped, bleak and cold, on the second inaugural day. But crowds stood patiently before the Capitol building. When the President appeared, they cheered wildly. At that instant the sun broke through and the wide plaza gleamed warmly. Many thought it a divine omen for good.

The inaugural address was deeply religious. Passages sounded like the verses from Isaiah that Tilly Johnston had heard Abe reciting in the woods near Pigeon Creek so long ago. The Bible had been Lincoln's guide in writing this address: he needed God's word more than the writings of statesmen if he was to help the country now. People listened in hushed silence. His closing words would be long remembered: "With malice toward none; with charity for all; with firmness in the right, as God gives us the strength to see the right, let us strive on to finish the work that we are in; to bind up the nation's wounds; to care for him who shall have borne the battle and for his widow, and his orphan—to do all which may achieve and cherish a just and lasting peace, among ourselves, and with all nations."

Later in March the President planned a little journey down the Potomac aboard the *River Queen*. Mrs. Lincoln and Tad went along, and Robert's fiancée. Robert was a captain on Grant's staff. They would see Robert, of course, and the general. Lincoln had liked Grant since that first meeting at the reception. He could talk frankly to him. The order to Sherman to come and meet with Grant and Lincoln was not generally known, but he was there.

On April 2nd, five days after Lincoln had conferred with Grant and Sherman, Richmond fell. Jefferson Davis and his cabinet hurriedly left the city; Lee's army gave up hope of defending the Confederate capital, and the Union general, Weitzel, was marching to take charge. The end of the long war could not be more than a few days away.

As soon as torpedoes were removed from the river, the President with Admiral Porter as escort, proceeded to Richmond. Lincoln wished to make a personal inspection.

This visit to the fallen city, which he had never seen, must have been one of the big moments in Abraham Lincoln's life. It was no formal entrance, just a walk with Tad to the mansion Jefferson Davis had vacated. A few black men were working on the wharf; as Lincoln and Tad walked from the boat, one recognized him.

"Glory Hallelujah!" the man shouted and ran to kneel before the President.

"Don't kneel to me!" Lincoln exclaimed. "You must kneel to God only!" But the man did not move.

" 'Scuse us, sir, we mean no disrespect . . . we mean all love and gratitude." Others ran to kneel, too, and they began to sing a hymn. It was with difficulty that Lincoln moved forward. Up the streets, as far as he could see were singing, shouting people.

The tall man walked slowly, holding his son's hand. Tad was twelve now, but small for his age. He was not afraid; his eyes sparkled, and he smiled. The President's face showed gentleness and concern. White people, peeping from shuttered windows, looked at him, astonished. Was this man the monster of the dreadful tales they had heard? He looked like a friendly neighbor coming to visit!

When the crowd became too great, Lincoln spoke again.

"I have but little time to spare," he told them. "I want to see your capital and must return at once to Washington to secure for you that liberty which you seem to prize so highly." So they let him move on.

Six days later, April 9th, 1865, General Lee surrendered, and generous peace terms were signed. Men could go to their homes and be safe as long as they did nothing against the Federal government.

There was a roar in Washington when these terms were known. They were "far too easy," it was said. And how did it happen, many asked, that both Grant and Sherman wrote the peace agreement in almost identical words? Politicians rushed to complain to the President. No one seemed to remember the conference on the *River Queen*. That trip had not been publicized.

"It's too late for a change, gentlemen," Mr. Lincoln told them firmly. "Our generals have announced terms which have been accepted. Now we must stand by our given word." Thus he showed himself to be a master politician.

On the afternoon of the fourteenth of April the President held a long and important cabinet meeting. Plans for the government of the South were informally discussed. Let private citizens go about business unmolested, the members advised, if they committed no hostile act against the government. Put war frictions aside. Let departments of government, the post office, and the treasury begin to work as best they could as though the South had never rebelled.

General Grant had met with the cabinet. As the meeting adjourned the President invited the general and his wife to be his guests at the theater that evening. But they were leaving the city and had to decline the honor.

The day was fine. After the meeting the President and Mrs. Lincoln went for a drive, alone. He talked of their future plans. "Mary," he said, "we have had a hard time of it since we came to Washington, but the war is over, and with God's blessing we may hope for four years of peace and happiness; then we will go back to Illinois and pass the rest of our lives in quiet."

Planning happily, they drove home to supper.

CHAPTER NINETEEN

APRIL 15, 1865

Visitors detained the President at the White House; so he and Mrs. Lincoln and their guests, Major Rathbone and his fiancée, were late in arriving at the theater that evening. The place was crowded; many in the audience were returning soldiers who had come in the hope of seeing their President. When Lincoln appeared, the play stopped and the band struck up "Hail to the Chief." The audience rose and cheered. The President bowed, and the play went on.

At noon that very day, John Wilkes Booth, a mad fanatic favoring the South, had heard that Lincoln was to attend the theater. He promptly

Abraham Lincoln's home in Springfield.

made plans for a deed that had been in his mind for some time.

About ten o'clock that evening he left his horse by the rear door of the theater and went to the hallway by the President's box. He carried with him a knife and a pistol. Sneaking into the box, he fired directly at the back of Lincoln's head.

Major Rathbone grabbed Booth, and was terribly cut in the arm. Booth shook the major off and leaped to the stage. The shot, then the leap, made many think that this was a part of the play. They were uneasy, but not frightened, until Major Rathbone shouted.

"Stop him! He has shot the President!"

The audience stared in horror. The theater was in wild confusion. Booth had caught his spur on a flag draped over the box; he fell on the stage and broke his leg. But the uncertainty of the audience gave him the chance to regain his balance, reach his horse, and gallop away.

In the President's box it was seen at once that Lincoln was fatally hurt. Doctors came. He was tenderly carried to a home across the street. Members of the cabinet, more doctors, his son Robert, and dozens of friends hurried to offer aid. But the man they wanted to save was injured beyond hope of recovery. After hours of unconsciousness, the President died about seven o'clock on the morning of April 15th.

By that hour, grieving crowds thronged Washington streets grabbing extra editions of newspapers which printed the awful news in great black letters:

EXTRA
THE PRESIDENT SHOT AT
THE THEATRE LAST EVENING

DEATH
OF
THE PRESIDENT

Black-bordered columns told the sad story. All over the country wires and presses were worked overtime carrying the news. People wept openly as they met on the street. The President's death was a shocking blow to the nation. The South lost a friend it hardly knew. The country lost a wise and experienced guide it sorely needed.

Services were held in the White House on Tuesday and among the Bible verses read were some phrases that told people's thoughts better than commonplace words:

"Man is cut down as a flower. Yet death may be swallowed up in victory."

Then began the long, sad journey back to the prairie state.

Lincoln's fellow countrymen wanted to pay personal tribute to their fallen hero, so arrangements were made for many stops—in New York, Philadelphia, Cleveland, Chicago, and other places. The black-draped train crept across the country between rows of weeping citizens. Cities, shrouded in crepe, echoed to the sound of funeral dirges, and ordinary business was suspended during two weeks of mourning. The final rites were held in Springfield on the fourth of May.

All this while the newspapers were filled with accounts of Lincoln's life. They recounted his hope of saving the Union, his faith, his hard work, his good judgment, and his kindness. He was a friend of all, the papers said, North and South, slave and free, and never had a man had higher ideals for his country.

Years have passed. And with each changing season the figure of Abraham Lincoln has grown. People have seen that his genius was many-sided. He chose law and politics for his lifework, but he might have been an actor: his sense of timing was perfect, and he had that gift for mimicry. Or he might have been a writer: he wrote poetry and satire as well as his excellent speeches. Instead he had poured all his gifts into the work he cared for most, political life. The stirring times in which he lived rewarded him with enduring fame.

In time he became the symbol of the American dream, the backwoods boy who, uneducated and lacking wealth and influence, won the highest office in the land. And he had not won by lucky political chance alone but by his honesty, dignity, and kindness. At a time when he might have gained popularity he stood stanchly for what he believed was true; when he might have compromised and had an easier entrance into the White House, he held to his given word.

The boy Abe Lincoln had pondered on the Declaration of Independence in Azel Dorsey's school and had memorized the stirring words, *All men are created equal.*

The grown man Abraham Lincoln had learned that men are not equal in all ways. He would never be as rich

LINCOLN'S OTHER ACCOMPLISHMENTS

Abraham Lincoln is best known, of course, for being the president to preserve the Union of States and abolish slavery. But he was responsible for many other accomplishments that still have impact on us today.

1. He reinforced the idea that the duty of the Executive Branch of government is to enforce the laws enacted by Congress. He did not believe that a President should actively steer the laws themselves but simply enforce them. To this day, this is a principle the Republican Party champions.

2. He signed the Homestead Act, which gave millions of acres of government-owned land to settlers at low cost. This helped develop the western territories very quickly, creating the nation we know today.

3. He signed the Morrill Land-Grant Colleges Act, providing the lands for colleges and universities in each state.

4. He supported the creation of the transcontinental railroad through the Pacific Railway Act.

5. In 1861, he created the first U.S. income tax by signing the Revenue Act.

6. He led the creation of a national banking system through the National Banking Act of 1862.

7. He made Thanksgiving a national holiday, not just a regional New England celebration.

Tickets to Ford's Theater.

The box in which assassin John Wilkes Booth shot Abraham Lincoln during the president's visit to Ford's Theatre in Washington, D.C.

as Senator Douglas; neither would Douglas be as tall as Lincoln. The Declaration did not promise impossibilities. Its signers were forming a new government. They wrote down what they proposed men's rights should be under the law. The document they wrote declared a man's right to live, to be free, and to try to be happy.

Abraham Lincoln gave his life to keep united a country dedicated to that ideal for men and women of every race and every creed.

★ CAST OF CHARACTERS ★

ABRAHAM LINCOLN
The 16th President
of the United States.

MARY TODD LINCOLN
Abraham Lincoln's wife, born in
Lexington, Kentucky.

JOHN T. STUART
Abraham Lincoln's first law partner;
the man credited with getting Lincoln
interested in the law.

MENTOR GRAHAM
An influential teacher of Abraham Lincoln's
during Lincoln's young adult years in New
Salem, Illinois.

MAJOR GENERAL
GEORGE MEADE
Leader of the Army of the Potomac at
the Battle of Gettysburg.

GENERAL
ULYSSES S. GRANT
Commanding General of the United
States Army from 1860 to 1864 and later
18th President of the United States.

STEPHEN A. DOUGLAS
U.S. representative and senator
from Illinois and candidate
for the presidency in 1860.

JOSHUA SPEED
A close friend of Lincoln's and
his partner in ownership of a
general store in New Salem, Illinois.

WILLIAM HERNDON
A fellow employee at Joshua Stuart's law firm,
Lincoln and Herndon formed their own law
firm in Springfield, Illinois, in 1844.

WILLIAM SEWARD
Although a political rival to Lincoln for the
party presidential nomination in 1860, Seward
was named Secretary of State by Lincoln.

GENERAL ROBERT E. LEE
Commanding general of the Army of Northern
Virginia and the most important military leader
of the Confederacy.

JOHN WILKES BOOTH
American stage actor and Confederate
sympathizer who assassinated
President Lincoln.

★ TIMELINE ★

1809
FEBRUARY 12
Abraham Lincoln is
born to Thomas and
Nancy Hanks Lincoln,
in Hardin Country,
Kentucky.

1831
Abraham leaves the
family, settling in
New Salem, Illinois,
at age 22.

1830
The Lincoln
family moves to
Illinois.

1819
DECEMBER 2
Thomas Lincoln
remarries to Sarah
Bush Johnson,
giving the Lincoln
children a beloved
stepmother.

1816
The Lincoln
family moves
to Indiana.

1832
Lincoln
becomes a
partner in a
small general
store in New
Salem, Illinois.

1818
OCTOBER 5
Abraham's mother,
Nancy, dies of
milk sickness.
DECEMBER 3
Illinois becomes
the 21st U.S. state.

1834
Lincoln wins
election as a state
representative.

1859
Lincoln loses
a senate race
to Stephen A.
Douglas.

1865
On April 15,
Abraham
Lincoln is
assassinated by
John Wilkes
Booth at Ford's
Theater in
Washington,
D.C.

1858
Lincoln delivers his
"House Divided" speech
at the Republican
Presidential Convention.

1857
In the Dred-Scott
Decision, the Supreme
Court rules that slaves
have no rights as
citizens.

1836
Lincoln is elected to
the Bar in Illinois
and begins practicing
law. He moves to
Springfield, Illinois.

1854
Lincoln gives
political speeches
opposing slavery;
he runs for a U.S.
Senate seat as a
Whig but loses.

1864
Lincoln is
elected to
a second
term.

1846
Lincoln wins
election to
U.S. House of
Representatives
and serves a two-
year term.

1860
Lincoln is nominated
for the presidency by the
Republican Party and wins
with a minority of the
popular vote to become
the 16th President of the
United States.

1861
Seven Southern states declare that
they are seceding from the United
States. On April 12, shots are fired
by Confederate troops at Union
troops at Fort Sumter, beginning
the Civil War.

1863
In January, Lincoln signs the
Emancipation Proclamation.
Confederate General Robert E. Lee
routs General Hooker at Battle of
Chancellorville in May. In July, Lee is
badly defeated by General Meade at the
Battle of Gettysburg. On November 19,
Lincoln delivers the Gettysburg Address.

INDEX